When Trouble Comes

Discovering the Themes in the Story of Your Life

Dr. Edward Wallach

www.Dr.EdwardWallach.com

Published in the United States of America
Two Suns Press

ISBN: 978-0-9850928-8-7
Library of Congress No. 2015938664

DEDICATION

This book is dedicated to all the people who want to understand and improve their lives so that they will experience less drama and trouble and have more success and happiness.

ACKNOWLEDGMENTS

To Colleen Wallach, my wife and best friend, for her unconditional love, advice and support.

To Dr. Leah Lagos-Wallach and Keith Wallach, Esq. for their advice, ideas, and continued support. To Dr. Steven Wallach for his counsel.

And my thanks to my editor and publisher, Janet Cunningham, Ph.D., who was instrumental with the whole process of helping this book come together.

TABLE OF CONTENTS

INTRODUCTION

Would you like to learn how to be happy? Being happy doesn't mean that you can totally eliminate trouble and problems from your life. In order to be happy, it is important to first learn how to handle the trouble and drama that is a part of life. Everyone, sooner or later, has some sort of experience filled with trouble. Sometimes it is just random trouble and sometimes we unintentionally or intentionally invite the trouble. Sometimes the trouble keeps repeating itself and we don't know why.

Did you ever, for a split-second, think that it wasn't a good idea to do something or get involved with someone and you didn't listen to yourself? People do this with the idea that it really won't lead to having too much trouble.

Did it ever occur to you that some people—whether they are aware of it or not—start fights when they feel anxious? Some people prefer to be angry rather than anxious because it is a more comfortable state.

Have you ever given into your guilt feelings even when you knew it might cause trouble? Did you know that just because you feel guilty, it doesn't mean that you have done something wrong? Feelings are not facts; they are inner emotions.

Should we accept that when people have trouble with marriage, relationships, raising and educating children, health, food or eating disorders that these experiences are just accidents or just meant to be? Or is it an excuse not to take action to improve the situation?

People want stress out of their lives so that they can be happy and contented. Let's *first* learn what trouble can be all about and how to handle it. This, in turn, can reduce or eliminate stress which can yield a more contented and happy life. I hope to *Emotionally Educate* you that trouble can be turned into a positive experience as I plan to teach you throughout this book.

As you read this book, you can understand that some of your difficulty could be related to your *Life Story*. The type of unrest you might have usually follows a *Theme* to how much you felt cared for or not cared for by others. The more uncaring feelings in your life essentially reflect the amount of trouble you will probably encounter.

The chapters include short stories showing how unresolved themes are constantly being replayed in a distorted manner throughout life and can hamper one's dreams. These stories demonstrate how a person investigates the underlying truth behind the causes of his trouble. They also offer examples demonstrating how you can handle various forms of trouble.

Keep in mind that a major key to conquering misfortune is (1) to discover and understand the *Themes* in your *Life Story* and (2) to comprehend the fact that you can't—nor should you—control how you feel…only how you act. No one is immune from it for very long because nothing stays the same; everything changes sooner or later.

Some people develop more difficulty than others, and some look like they don't have any trouble but they do; these challenges are a part of life. Sometimes you can see unrest coming, sometimes it sneaks up on you before you know it, and sometimes it snowballs without you having any control. When you can step back and look at your life, you will see that you are often the architect of your own misfortune.

Most people unintentionally re-establish the same environment they grew up in because it is familiar. It is not easy to recognize, yet the past is etched in your mind. You find yourself repeating the same difficulty over and over until you comprehend and accept your trouble, shift your behavior, and move on.

This book is based largely on my knowledge, experience and innovative ideas that I have figured out and tested over years of practice doing psychotherapy, teaching and in my personal life. Trouble can actually be an opportunity for emotional and spiritual growth. Difficultly in your life can be a voyage of personal discovery.

After reading this book, you can develop an understanding and become your own archeologist, ready to excavate hidden troubles that hold you back from success. The more you understand your *Life Story*, the better prepared you are to handle the future. So please come with me on a journey of self-discovery and a more enriched life.

When Trouble Comes

Discovering the Themes in the Story of Your Life

Trouble Comes randomly or when we are stuck or unhappy and success comes when we grow emotionally, mentally, and possibly heal physically. Our readiness can lead us to discovering our *Life Story* and moving out of repetitive patterns learned early in life.

Trouble Comes when
- we don't *feel our feelings*, suppressing them in order to make others happy
- we act out of fear about another's reaction or behavior
- we act on how we feel rather than what makes sense

Trouble Comes when
- we don't recognize that we are repeating a pattern over and over…drawing people or circumstances to us that replicate our experiences in childhood
- we have fear that we will repeat the actions or marriages of our parents

Trouble Comes when
- we are unable to view our past with honesty…creating an *illusion* of happy childhood even though it is not our actual experience
- we are fearful that acknowledging the true actions and behaviors of those who we expect to love us will bring even more pain

Trouble Comes when
- our relationships include painful memories and repetitive patterns of others in authority positions
- we cannot speak up for our own needs

**Trouble Comes when
we cannot recognize or acknowledge
our own feelings or emotions**

Success Comes when
- we learn about *Emotional Education* and practice it.
- we discover our *Life Story* and choose the themes we want to continue to live and those parts that we are ready to release.
- we stick to productive goals no matter how we feel.

What are the Themes of Your Life?

Recognizing your *Life Story* can be the first step to more joy and peace in your life. After reading this book, you may discover that the *Theme of Your Life* falls into one or more of the following categories. You might add to the list according to your particular experiences. Our experiences in childhood and the relationships between us and our mothers[1], fathers, siblings, and others play a large part in the attitudes, beliefs, and behavior that we carry into adulthood. Unknowingly, we repeat these patterns over and over.

Some common perceived *Themes* are:

- Abandonment
- Favorite (or un-favorite) in the family
- The intelligent (or un-intelligent) one in the family
- The pretty/handsome one (or "ugly duckling")
- Born for success or headed for failure in life
- I need to protect mommy/daddy
- I need to make mommy/daddy happy
- I have to be good to be accepted by others (or I'm the "black sheep" in the family
- Caught in the Life Story, or neediness, of your mother/father
- Unable to express emotions in the family structure
- Inability to feel one's emotions and/or stored emotions, such as anger
- Abusive mother or father, siblings, etc.

---

[1] Mother and father used throughout the book can also refer to other family members, guardians, etc.

- Guilt
- I have to take care of myself; there is no one who can help me
- Fear of being like mother/father or fear of repeating their marriage patterns

And perhaps the most powerful:

- I am loved or I am unloved.

BECOMING A WINNER

Look at your trouble as a mirror showing you an aspect of yourself that you need to explore and improve. After the exploration, you can have the potential to accomplish almost anything you desire.

Trouble can be viewed as a positive learning tool in life to grow emotionally. Although you may blame bad breaks or the bad economy, the only one standing in your way from achieving your dreams is you.

You have excuses for why you cannot achieve your goals such as "It's too hard...too frightening... or just not the right time;" however, the real hurdle to your success is you.

Explore trouble as a path to understand your personal enigmas which are holding you back from being a winner. Everyone has hidden trouble in his life, but turmoil has the ability to appear without warning and cause problems. Trouble can force you to take a look at those parts of your personality that you have been trying to avoid. These hidden areas are at the root of your difficulties. When you bring your troubles out into the daylight, you will realize that there is nothing to be afraid of. You have the ability to conquer negative, unproductive feelings. You can develop the ability to become the leader by understanding the Themes in your Life Story. You can become your own advisor in solving your problems.

Doubt is a feeling in your mind that has the ability to halt your movement forward. Themes in your Life Story tend to form limiting beliefs about what you cannot achieve. You, then, assume those falsehoods are truths.

Believing you are not successful feels safer than searching inside to reach the truth of why you

1

cannot push yourself to improve. Avoiding this inner search, in the long run, is a path that leads you into trouble.

Remind yourself that your fears reflect only what could go wrong and not what could go right.

> *Your insecurities seem real*
> *because your mind seeks only evidence that supports*
> *these negative feelings and ignores evidence*
> *that these thoughts could be wrong.*

Your mind creates excuses because they make life comfortable. If you surround yourself with these feelings, you will buy into these attitudes, diminishing your chance of success. If you focus on negative outcomes, you will live a nonproductive life.

Self-pity is another inflicted belief, and it is a strong drug to overcome. When faced with trouble, don't immediately act on your feelings. Take time to evaluate the situation and act on what makes sense, not on how you feel. Don't say, "Why me?" Don't hide behind this excuse. Your feelings give you information about what is going on in your environment. Don't get side tracked with self-pity; aim for your goals.

Overcoming your failures and negative experiences isn't an easy task. This book explains how you grow from understanding why these experiences happen and how to stop repeating them.

Negative experiences should be viewed as a learning lesson to move into a positive environment. In order to get healthier, you must take this journey. There is no quick fix that makes life easier, but you can eventually break bad habits that are associated with your Life Story.

Most of us believe that familiarity and comfort are very important, but this concept is not entirely correct. Repeating what you have done many times can be comfortable, but your comfort zone may not be compatible with achievement. You may prefer the safety of your comfort area, but may pay a huge price for this safety. Trying new paths is one of the most effective ways to happiness and success.

The human brain is stimulated by discovery. Successfully coping with the unfamiliar can provide a high level of performance. A life without risk is a life without excitement, without feelings of accomplishment, and without any hope of fulfilling dreams.

> *Your greatest happiness and success in life can usually be found on the other side of fear.*

Another hidden hardship is the bad habit of comparing your existence to those of other people who are successful; this thought process only makes the world seem unfair. It creates conflict for you and is a form of self-sabotage.

> *Even if your problems are not one-hundred percent your fault, they are one-hundred percent your responsibility.*

View these problems as challenges to overcome. You have the ability to correct your life—do not think otherwise.

Attitude is more important than facts and our attitude towards our troubles define us.

Life is a team sport between the past, the present, and the future. Comprehending your trouble wakes you up to question your motivations and makes you conscious of what you are doing to yourself. Open the door in your mind to understand your Themes and your tribulations as they relate to your inability to become a winner. Take charge and walk through the door for a better way of life.

If you do not overcome your trouble, it will rule you throughout your life. You have a great adaptability that enables you to be a survivor in any situation. Approach life with power and positive emotions not excuses, and you can always find the bright side.

This book will act as your glasses to see life more clearly, and your goals may not seem so far in the distance.

BEGINNINGS OF MY EMOTIONAL EDUCATION

My internship program in graduate school was the start of my voyage into understanding more about individuals and how they act when trouble appears. It was also, in a very real sense, the beginnings of my *Emotional Education*, both professionally and personally.

I was on my quest to become a therapist. That included learning and applying principles which I was learning in school. Learning from a textbook is the basis to start; however, discovering ideas on my own was enlightening. Textbooks rarely addressed the ideas that I found myself using in my practice.

> *The amount of trouble a person has in life is directly related to how much they feel cared for or how much they don't feel cared for.*

I quickly learned that difficulties in the present can be rooted in feelings and actions from our *Life Story* or from our parents' *Life Stories* that are thrust upon us.

During the time I was in school, according to the school's regulations, a supervisor helped me in my new role. My female supervisor was in her forties and well educated in the mental-health field. She was a likable woman from an Ivy League school. In the mid-1970's, I carried two caseloads consisting of adolescents and their parents.

My younger clients' intellectual functioning ranged from mildly to moderately retarded, and they demonstrated severe forms of emotional disturbance, ranging from acting-out behavior to ideas not based in reality.

The clinic was on the west side of Harlem in New York City. This was a neighborhood filled with blue-collar workers and many of the residents were single mothers. The room in the building where I was going to practice had a sterile appearance. The quarters were small and painted white with a metal desk and cabinets. There were chairs with very little cushioning on the seats which made sitting for a period of time uncomfortable.

My office didn't have a window and the only lighting came from the bright florescent tubes anchored from the ceiling panels. The room looked like an operating suite, and there was a cold atmosphere radiating from the walls.

My supervisor stated that it was my responsibility not to pass judgment on my clients; it was my duty to help them understand themselves more clearly by verbalizing the origin of their difficulty. With my first client and his mother, I was able to help them grow as a family. My second client helped me understand the feelings of losing control over a situation with abandonment issues. Perhaps the importance of one's life can be summed up with the impact his life has on others. These clients' lives impacted my life, and I touched theirs.

JOEY'S THEME OF BEING CAUGHT IN THE LIFE STORY OF HIS MOTHER

The first client I met was a fifteen-year-old boy and his mother who lived in the Harlem neighborhood. Joey was a large-framed teenager who was dressed in a clean blue shirt and jeans. His mother was a woman whose hard life showed in the lines on her face. She dressed simply in a plain cotton dress and appeared to

6

look like Joey's grandmother more than his mother. She was a woman in her forties but she looked older than her years.

I saw Joey and his mother for individual appointments after each other. His mother explained to me, "I don't want to lose him to the streets. He is the baby of my family." She continued, "One of my children was killed on the streets of Harlem by random gun fire, one is a prostitute, and the other one is a drug addict. I want to save Joey from the family's fate. I want him to grow up to be a good citizen."

Joey's mother certainly did not want to relive unwelcome ghosts; she wanted to move ahead in life. Yet it was hard for her to emotionally break from her personal past difficulties.

She also talked about her own life and her childhood. When she was a young girl, she lived in poverty in the South. At the time, she was cleaning houses for a living and could just afford the two-dollar fee per visit for herself and her son. Her son was diagnosed by the New York City Board of Education as a teenager of limited intelligence, and a child with severe acting-out behavior; therefore, he was placed by the Board of Education in a special school. The mother's goal in therapy was that she wanted him to behave, stay out of trouble in school and at home.

When I met Joey, I was expecting to see an uncooperative teenager who wasn't too intelligent but I was wrong. He came in, sat down, and clearly explained what he thought would help him. He said, "My problem is my mother won't buy me a bicycle. I believe my mother doesn't really love me and that is why she won't get me the bike." Furthermore, he reported when he doesn't believe that he is appreciated, he starts trouble or gets himself into a difficult situation.

He continued, "My mother always agrees to buy me a bike if I am well behaved. After I am good, she still doesn't get me the bike because she thinks I am going to misbehave again." He explained that it wasn't worth it to try to behave because his mother breaks her promise. He repeated his thought that the reasons behind his mother's behavior was that she didn't love him and she didn't believe in him.

When I met the mother the following week, we discussed the topic of the bicycle. She did agree with part of Joey's reasoning. She didn't buy a bike for him because she wasn't sure he would act correctly in school and at home. She did mention she cares a great deal about her son. As I continued to work with the mother, she agreed to get him the bicycle if she knew he would continue to be well-mannered.

After many sessions, she finally committed herself to the agreement; she would buy a bike for Christmas. I realized that it was hard emotionally for Mrs. K to give presents because she did not grow up with this concept.

I explained the arrangement to Joey. He said he would be on his best behavior until Christmas and see if he gets the present. He also emphasized, "You should listen to me because I am not going to get the bike because she doesn't love me."

Since September, I had been working on this dilemma of the bike. Before the holidays, the mother reported that her son was behaving both in school and at home. I wished them both a Merry Christmas and a Happy New Year. I was feeling confident that Joey would get his present.

8

After the holidays, we resumed. Mrs. K came in and stated that Joey had been suspended from school. She explained, "Upon his return from the winter vacation, he threw a chair at his teacher and wrecked the classroom." She never mentioned the bicycle.

I started to get suspicious, and asked how Joey enjoyed his bike. She reluctantly mentioned she didn't get it for him. The teenager had been right.

Therefore, Joey's acting-out behavior supported the fact that the teenager didn't feel cared for—he was acting out his anger, which he couldn't verbalize to his mother.

On an unintentional level, she was setting her son up for failure which was similar to her own childhood experiences.

Interestingly, through their story, I rediscovered my own past emotions that were similar to Joey's. My childhood dealt with similar unresolved issues of broken promises. I certainly knew how it felt when one takes an emotional beating. I worked through this by learning to create a positive environment for myself.

When Joey came in, he was quiet and he looked as if his world was coming to an end. I felt very uncomfortable hearing the words which I knew were coming. "I told you she wouldn't get me the bike."

I was trying to understand why she really didn't get him the gift. It had to do with the story of the mother's life. Her poor southern family couldn't afford to give her presents. Her family had a hard time keeping a roof over their heads and food on the table. As a single mother, Mrs. K was facing similar experiences. She was trying to keep her family together by cleaning houses and on an unintentional level, she was reliving her own childhood traumas.

I realized that for the mother to give her son a bike, I needed to give her some attention and compassion so that she could move away from her unresolved childhood emotions.

For many months, I encouraged her to talk about her difficult Life Story. Even though her sessions seemed confusing and lacked connection, every word led back to her upbringing and the unrest she faced. Her life was crowded by unfulfilled desires and memories which were all jumbled up in her mind. As a young girl, her parents loved her. Still, due to the circumstances her parents were never able to give her the gifts she dreamt of.

Unintentionally, Joey's mother needed to re-enact a Theme in her Life Story. If she explained to her son what her poor upbringing felt like, it wouldn't have an emotional impact on him.

Her behavior gave Joey similar feelings that the mother felt as a young girl. His mother was still tied up in the emotions she had as a child. Her past was reappearing and causing trouble.

After a year and a half in therapy, everything came to a head. When Joey couldn't experience his mother's love, he could not restrain himself from getting into serious trouble. Joey's acting-out behavior was demonstrated when he missed an appointment because he stole $5,000 from his sister's pimp and he was hiding out.

Mrs. K said, "The word on the street is to kill Joey, and I am scared." I listened to Mrs. K with concern about Joey's situation yet unable to free her from her doubts, her guilt, and her self-reproaches in one session,

I listened, hoping to guide her into a correct thought process. Nevertheless, I was not able to open avenues for relief or bring thoughts under control by the time the session ended. I didn't know what would happen in their therapy the following week.

When Joey showed up for his next appointment, he told me his mother returned the money. She pleaded for his life and it worked. I knew she cared for him, but Joey didn't feel the devotion his mother had for him. He never mentioned how his mother saved him from potential death and how much she loved him. He just stated that he was happy he didn't die.

Joey had a way of expressing his emotions to himself, as well as to me, which were not consistent with reality.

In therapy, the important aspects are emotions and what happens to them—are they revealed or are they hidden? Joey was having difficulty seeing the truth.

After months of listening to the mother's Life Story, I finally asked her to buy her son the bike. I thought she might be cooperative. Mrs. K decided that I was moved by her Life Story, and I was emotionally concerned by her plight. She felt special and understood, and this enhanced our relationship as a positive experience.

My theory finally worked after nurturing her for over a year. She bought him the bicycle that cost $50 which was her entire week's salary.

She reported that her son became a changed person because of the bike. Joey stated that he finally knew his mother loved him.

The most amazing occurrence happened the following week. Joey came in with a big smile on his face. He reported, "I was jumped while riding my new bike in the park." Instead of this being a negative

11

experience it turned into a positive one. He said, "This time my mother will take on extra work to buy me another bike."

The last day of our sessions, I saw them and he did get the bike. He was really feeling appreciated and his behavior at home and in school greatly improved. Both of them thanked me for helping them. Mrs. K also thanked me for assisting her to stop repeating her childhood experiences through Joey. She clearly understood the repetition concept and emerged from it.

> *Everyone has ungratified tensions stored up from his Life Story. Whether these feelings express themselves openly or not, it is always helpful to acknowledge these Themes and organize one's life accordingly.*

One needs to understand that gifts, when reasonable, are important for a child to feel appreciated. Most people know that actions speak louder than words, and in this case, the bicycle reflected the feeling of being cared for. When a person feels understood, the amount of trouble he encounters may decrease or the distress may stop completely.

GUY'S LIFE STORY OF INABILITY TO COMMUNICATE FEELINGS

Another teenager was assigned to me by my supervisor; the client's name was Guy, considered to be severely retarded. His mother brought the very friendly, eighteen-year old to talk to me. The first few weeks, he spent time explaining how I must be Wilt Chamberlain's brother. His association was the fact that the famous tall basketball player must have been my brother because I was tall like Chamberlain.

12

Most of the time, he was convinced I was Elvis Presley. He would come in and say, "Okay Elvis, let's sing Elvis' songs." I would follow his lead and sing songs with him.

His mother told me he was improving with his relationships with others, and I was very helpful. Whatever I was doing, she recommended that I should continue. I was using a concept of Emotional Education by joining him on his level.

Teaching children how to handle their feelings is as important, in my opinion, as teaching them how to work with letters, figures, and other intellectual concepts. They need to understand why they feel angry, melancholy, or tearful at times and what is healthful and socially appropriate for them to say and do in these states. The desirability of thinking and talking about troublesome feelings and the undesirability of discharging them in a social behavior are lessons which every person should learn in life.

> *When Emotional Education is not learned and experienced in childhood, it will follow a person into adulthood with troublesome consequences.*

I continued to work with Guy, from his emotional and mental status. That included helping him feel understood with nothing threatening to him. I used the concepts of Emotional Education throughout the entire therapy. For two years, Guy and I only sang songs, and there was very little verbalization between us. It was hard to get him to talk about his life because it appeared that he was living in a fantasy world and I became part of it.

My internship would be ending shortly and I thought it wouldn't matter to Guy if I was there or not. I believed, after all, that he wasn't really there himself. When I had two weeks left, I followed the protocol for leaving.

Guy came in and said, "Okay Elvis let's sing." Before we sang, I told him I had something to tell him. I said, "In two weeks I will meet with you for the last time. I will be leaving the clinic." He said, "Okay Elvis, let's sing Elvis' songs."

My supervisor felt that I shouldn't have any concerns about my departure because he was essentially not aware and would not miss me. I learned an important lesson about human behavior.

The next week he didn't keep his last appointment; this was the first time he had missed a session. His mother called the clinic and left a message with my supervisor.

When Guy was ironing his shirt as he always did in the morning, he turned the iron around and purposely held it on his arm to burn himself. He didn't have a history of violence because he never hurt anybody or himself in his life. He was a passive, kind person. His mother conveyed he was in the hospital with third degree burns and thanked me for all my help. He would not be returning for the last session.

I was shocked and beside myself with Guy's behavior. I had severely underestimated the impact I had on him. My supervisor agreed that it was certainly not a coincidence. The supervisor speculated Guy couldn't handle the separation, and must have felt it was his fault.

It became apparent to me that Guy had a problem in voicing his feelings, and he thought it was his fault. He probably felt he was a bad person who doesn't deserve friends, and he punished himself. This emotion of abandonment led him into hurting himself rather than expressing his emotions towards me.

A significant fact was taught to me through this negative experience. If a person feels unworthy, he might punish himself. Guy was unable to state his true emotions, and he was unable to adjust readily to changes in his environment.

Every individual has his[1] own volume in the book of life if he knows how to read it. Through this case, I learned that a therapist needs to talk about a termination date with the client and share the effect it will have on him or her personally. He needs to make the ending process as pleasant as possible; it should not be a quick closure. This also applies to everyone in life.

Guy's avoidance to discuss the ending took a toll on him. The skill of talking about termination should be employed some time before the actual end. The client did not want to talk about it, I was reluctant to discuss it, and I allowed the topic to be dropped.

It was a sign of my own ambivalence, and I learned not to relive this type of circumstance again. From this trouble, I learned a valuable lesson.

Guy was demonstrating he didn't have the appropriate behavior to open himself up to new possibilities of moving on and getting a new therapist. As in his past, he felt he was hopeless in this circumstance. He didn't realize he had the power to adjust to a new situation. He believed he couldn't face his new life because he didn't want the old one to change. He was comfortable with me as his therapist. In his inability to take control of his environment, he became a victim.

---

[1] The pronouns his/her, she/he, etc. are used interchangeably in this book.

> *Life spins out of control many times;*
> *you have the ability to accept it and to build a*
> *better, new life.*

Don't go by your previous life's script of disappointment and failure. You are not a victim of circumstances. I believe that I was helpful to the family who had a conflict over a bike. On the other hand, I felt terrible about the boy who burned himself.

I questioned myself: *What went right and what went wrong in these cases?* I learned that people who act as if they are not there and have limited intelligence should be taken seriously because they have feelings also.

As long as we do not criticize ourselves about a poor outcome, this thought-provoking process can be used to obtain information about how we make decisions. I realized that life is filled with many loose ends, and we must tie them together to examine the entire picture of the direction of our path to success.

Every day is a learning experience and even your trouble should be looked upon as a positive way to move forward. You might feel powerless and victimized because of the trouble you are facing. This is a common source of complaints among people. Take responsibility and face yourself in the cold harsh light of day.

When you realize you have the ability to put thoughts into positive actions, you do not have to continue with behavior which makes you a victim. Your actions shape your existence, and it is up to you to make your own world a better place in which to live.

Facing Problems

A problem is a perplexing question or circumstance that you are faced with and you might be uncertain about its solution. It can appear as a riddle or a puzzle which is hard to solve, and it can cause trouble for you and everyone who you know if you do not truly comprehend it.

You can break a pattern of doubtful behavior when you understand what is causing it, and many times another person's past problems can get impacted into your Life Story. I realized this fact when I took a part-time position as an adjunct instructor at Kingsborough Community College where I taught mental-health courses with an emphasis on an Emotional Education approach.

Instead of using the traditional teaching atmosphere in which the class faces the teacher and the chalkboard, I had my class members use face-to-face seating in a circle in which I was included. This atmosphere helped to facilitate all the members into the discussion. Although these adult students were not as impulsive as youngsters, some of their negative feelings towards authority figures ran as deep. One of my first assignments was teaching a course entitled, *Happiness Training,* which I developed.

A STUDENT'S LIFE STORY WITH A THEME
OF TRANSFERRING FEELINGS

On the first day of class, as I wrote my name on the chalkboard, a woman who I had never met shouted that she hated me. Looking at the woman who was in her thirties and well groomed, it would seem this behavior was atypical.

My inner thought was, *She must not be happy, and I shouldn't take that remark personally*. I asked her why she disliked me; she thought for a moment and answered, "I don't know why." Perplexed by my benign and helpful reaction to her verbal attack, she was not quite sure what to say, so I offered, "When you know, then let me know."

I was practicing Emotional Education in this situation. Emotional Education, as explained previously, is a concept in which the instructor (and/or parent) tries to understand the person and his thought process. Therefore, the instructor can work from the reference point of his student's emotional conduct. Also, Emotional Education aids the pupil in comprehending his own feelings.

A half hour into the lesson, she called out, "I detest you because you are tall." I thought, *Here we go again with this tall stuff*. I asked her, "What does the feeling of hate have to do with me being tall?" She couldn't answer.

Later on, she interrupted the lesson by telling me that she did not loathe me personally, but I reminded her of her first husband who was tall and she disliked him. She said, "I understand my negative feeling and I don't despise you anymore." In fact, she said she might like me.

This is an example of transferring troublesome feelings towards a stranger at first sight and repeating the story of one's life with an outsider. During the rest of the semester, I encouraged this pupil to verbalize her hostility and resentment. As my own training as a therapist had progressed over the years, I learned not to take verbal aggression personally, but to treat it as

18

the preferred vehicle some people have for communicating their inner feelings. Since the student experienced that I was accepting her emotions, she was able to function in the class.

> *Practice not taking the bait*
> *when people provoke you. Think about how you*
> *want to handle it.*

An author and former member of Congress commented that there are no hopeless situations...only men who have grown helpless about them. I knew that I was going to be a person who uses the word "can" throughout my life. The word "can" gives power to the user. You must get to know yourself and through this process you can get on with your life.

Understand your limitations and the limitations of your associates. This idea became apparent to me when I was teaching another education course entitled *Widows and Widowers.*

A GROUP THEME OF LOSS AND INDUCED FEELINGS

There were nine widows and one widower in the course. All the participants were much older than I. They had the same reaction as I had when I met them. We were thinking similar thoughts, "How can this young man possibly help with my bereavement?"

I knew the only way to help people is to get them to talk and describe their Life Stories. Luckily this group was talkative; they cooperated and talked about how they lost their loved ones within the last two to five years. They described how others were caring in the first six months. Yet, after that period of time, the concerned calls and visits drastically decreased.

Therefore, they felt abandoned for a second time. In the group setting, they felt better by verbalizing these feelings. They realized other people in the class were going through similar situations and their abandonment issues became diminished over time.

The next meeting continued with the Theme of feeling misunderstood and unloved. The class mentioned when they told close associates or family and friends that they were not doing well after their loved one's death, they received uncaring responses. The responses ranged from, "You have to get on with your life," or "You should take a trip." The group asked me why they encountered these statements.

I mentioned it was probably because the close associates didn't know what to say, and they felt uncomfortable about the topic. Also, I added that their peers found it difficult to listen to how they actually felt. By not dealing with it, the close colleagues and family members could insulate themselves from lonely emotions, and they spared themselves the hardship of feeling the loss of a loved one.

The group members did not realize that they were inducing these *death feelings* in their acquaintances; this made them uncomfortable. They began to understand why others were afraid to talk to them. The members noted that their troublesome emotions were so powerful that most of their peers were in denial that they could be faced with the death of a spouse.

Through the process of talking to others, the group members were able to feel understood. They were able to break down their problem into smaller units. They searched for the details. The members

20

helped one another add to their personal inventory from each other's experiences. Both negative and positive emotions helped the group to support each other. The members rehearsed new ways of handling old dilemmas, and they defined their new reality.

During the third session, many in the group began to cry about how much they missed their mates. After listening to them, I began to feel physically ill. The members noticed my behavior, and were ready to stop their mourning to take care of me. I reassured them that it was just a case of indigestion, and it would soon pass.

The truth was that they were inducing the feelings of abandonment and death in me. Being a survivor of my parents' abuse, once again I found myself in distress. I knew if I could finish listening to the group, I could make it home and my wife would take care of me. My hidden past was reappearing without my consent.

I drove home from the class fighting off the sensation of fainting, and I collapsed on the floor of my house. My wife helped by encouraging me to talk about my experience with the class. I slowly felt better and the next day I was fine.

I asked myself, *What happened to me last night?* A few days later, it dawned on me: I was feeling the nonverbal part of the class' story that they were not putting into words. They felt like dying and were not expressing it.

When I started the next class, the group expressed concern that I was all right. I replied, "Yes; however, I need help because I am indirectly getting vibrations from some members in the group who want to die." No one in the class appeared to be shocked by my statement. I asked them if I was right about the desire.

There was dead silence in the room for about thirty seconds. One woman burst out crying because she constantly thinks about dying and joining her husband. The widower in the group said, "I feel the same but I stop myself because my wife made me promise I would remarry after she died." The other members all verbalized that they thought and felt like dying on a regular basis because their loneliness was overwhelming. The process of talking instead of keeping such feelings inside helped them overcome negative feelings which had been causing distress.

Most members never told close associates about this death feeling. They thought if they revealed this emotion, family and friends would think they were losing their minds. One woman confirmed this idea. She mentioned to her daughter she felt like dying, and her daughter insisted she see a psychiatrist for medication and suicide prevention.

The mother was mourning over her husband. She had no plans for dying; she just missed her husband. After hearing her daughter's response, the mother never talked to her again about her true emotions. The daughter unintentionally insulated herself from her mother's problem.

The last day of class, the members had a party because they felt they learned aspects about themselves and about each other. They had a common bond. The group's termination was not abrupt because they realized that the term was ending. None of its members felt that I abandoned them. They spent their time operating independently and talking about meeting

22

informally again. I thanked them for assisting me in dealing with the worrisome feelings I had experienced in our meetings.

The group helped me confirm my belief that one may experience emotions from others when the Story of his Life is somewhat parallel. The intensity of these emotions can be directly related to the amount of caring or the amount of non-caring you might have had in your past.

Everyone in the world is guaranteed that dying will be part of his life, but no one wants to think about it. We try to shield ourselves from this topic and go on with our lives.

HELEN'S THEME OF LOSS

The induced feelings of death and the uncertainty of life were quite evident on September 11, 2001—that is when the NYC World Trade Center fell to terrorism. People all over the world had a hard time insulating themselves to this heartbreaking situation.

Two of my clients—a divorced mother and her daughter—were directly involved in this situation. Over the years, I had made great progress with them, but September 11 changed all of that. The daughter who was 26 years old died; she worked in the second tower, and she perished without any warning to her family.

Helen was faced with the unexpected death of her child. She mentioned to me how she experienced a similar sentiment with her close associates as the group of widows and widowers. No one wanted to listen to her misfortune.

23

Since Helen didn't have a husband, her mother was her closest associate. Her mother repeatedly reminded Helen that she had another child and to get on with her life.

Of course, having another child couldn't erase the death of her daughter. My client was able to surface her feelings in an appropriate therapeutic setting. If this had not occurred, her emotions would have been hidden in her mind and heart. Therefore, this hidden emotion could have caused her a great deal of harm.

Helen asked if she would ever feel better. I explained, "The loss of your child is like having a phantom limb. It is gone but you feel that the limb is still there. Sometimes you even go to touch the limb just as if you didn't lose it." The mind has difficulty making adjustment, especially with a sudden death, but the mind will eventually adjust to the loss. It is hard for an individual to feel life is fair when your child is killed for no apparent reason.

Even years later after this tragedy, Helen expressed many times that she felt unable to move on from her great loss.

She related that she would get a call from New York City that they found another body part, and she had to relive the nightmare again.

Helen felt it was impossible for her to get her life together; she was stuck in September 11. The news press and media were constantly talking about the destruction of human lives and this did not make her feel better—it just reminded her of her tragedy. It became difficult for her to move beyond September 11 because the medical examiner and the media supplied her with induced troublesome pain.

Helen stated, "As soon as I come to some-sort-of-terms with the situation, others stir up my heartache of the horror over my child's death. I start to wonder again if she suffered."

Having a true audience within your family and close associates for expressing how you feel is necessary. If that isn't available, speaking to another person is valuable, as long as the other party can stay reasonably objective. Keep in mind who your audience is when you share your feelings. Helen said that she would receive fifty or more phone calls a week. I said, "Enjoy it while you have it." After time, fewer people called. The few that did call were able to listen to her feelings. I mentioned if she wanted the others to call her again, she should create a positive environment by letting them know she is feeling okay and move the conversation forward. Her goal was accomplished; she played the game and felt it was worth it.

Helen mentioned to me that talking on a one-to-one basis helped her express all the angry, negative feelings which were pent up inside of her. She acknowledged that I was a caring person who would listen and not judge her emotions. She was able to move on; still, every September 11th she relives her nightmare, fortunately with less intensity.

> *When you are faced with trouble, don't focus on "Why me?" feelings. Take the time and effort to think about your Life Story before moving forward.*

Only move in the direction of a helpful, productive life. Act on what makes sense to improve your well-being. Aim for your goals. You have the ability not to repeat the terrible period in your life.

You have the ability to re-define your new reality.

MOVING AHEAD

Your life is similar to a novel. You must move on to a new chapter to expand your horizons. In literature, if the writer stands still, the plot cannot move forward and it ends.

Self-therapy is tuning into your struggles in order to move on with your life. An honest look at memories and searching for your needs assists in transporting you to the next chapter of your life.

(1) Think about what Themes keep coming up during the Story of your Life.
(2) Acknowledge and accept your feelings.
(3) Put your emphasis on positive feelings; avoid focusing on the negative.
(4) Practice no longer feeling sorry for yourself or being a victim.
(5) Stick to your goal no matter how you feel.

Denial makes a deep impression in your mind and body. Accepting your own personal thoughts aids you to step into reality and gives you the power to grow. You must not try to relive the worst moments in your life. These terrible thoughts should be verbalized and not acted out.

> *If your mind is filled with negativity,*
> *this attitude goes out into the atmosphere,*
> *and it will come back to you in the form of unrest.*

This concept of positive outlook was highlighted for me a few years ago when I read an article on longevity in a major newspaper. The researchers studied a group of centurions to try to figure out how they had managed to live over a hundred years. By this time, many of the centurions had experienced major tragic events in their lives such as the death of a spouse, the death of siblings, the death of close friends, and the deaths of some of their children.

Apparently the researchers were expecting to find and prove that these centurions had always exercised, had good cholesterol levels, had good blood pressure levels, and had never smoked.

To their surprise, some of these individuals experienced poor exercise habits, had poor cholesterol levels, had poor blood pressure levels, and some were smokers. The researchers were amazed by the results. How did these people live beyond a hundred years?

The researchers did discover one major factor that these elderly people had in common. It was their ability to deal in a positive manner with whatever difficulty they encountered during their life span. They would encounter the experience, get through it, and not dwell on it. They were able to redirect themselves into a healthier environment, and they were truly survivors of life.

The idea behind the centurions' long life span seems to be their ability not to repeat their negative Life Stories. This idea is to lean towards the light and not the dark side. It was their ability to redirect their lives for the better, to accept the past and to move on. They did not let the past define them as persons.

The law of attraction,
whether it is positive or negative,
influences all of us.
What we think and feel many times comes back
to us in an experience.

Working with my clients, I re-learned this concept. It is my desire that you may relate to one or some of the following stories. Hopefully when this happens, you will have a better understanding as to what to do when trouble comes.

Or, perhaps you may be the one who brings difficulty to others. Hopefully, you will be able to emerge from whatever your conflict and go to the next level by understanding and conquering your trouble.

The most pronounced example of the concept of negativity, denial, and fear occurred with an attractive female client with big green eyes; she was approximately forty-five years old. Mrs. D came to my office for only two sessions. In my personal observation, she really didn't want to try to understand her need for causing adversity or even try to correct it. Looking back, I am sure the trouble had to do with her Life Story.

Mrs. D came to my office just two weeks after her husband died. She explained, "I hated my husband for twenty years and only told him this fact before his death."

She continued with her story, "Two weeks before his death was our wedding anniversary; my husband gave me flowers and told me he loved me. He asked me if I loved him. I guess he had a doubt in his mind about my affection."

She responded to him by saying, "I've hated you for our entire marriage, and I hope you drop dead." He died right in front of her as soon as she spoke those words.

Mrs. D asked me, "Did I kill him with my remark?" I replied, "He didn't have to cooperate with you." Her husband appeared to be a person who had a quick, impulsive reaction to this situation—or it could have been a slow growing reaction which finally released itself with its stored up negative energy.

I didn't work with this woman long enough to understand her Life Story. It appears she had the ability to make her husband feel he should die, and the short time I worked with her I felt she had a temperament to make one feel uncomfortable being in her world. She induced in me a sense that she had the ability to harm a person emotionally and physically.

A person's thoughts and feelings can be very potent aspects in life. Confrontational thoughts, words, and emotions can cause distress and illness if not handled properly.

> *One of the key aspects in handling negative emotions is to understand the fact that you can't control how you feel but you can handle how you act.*

Therefore, feel all your emotions and thoughts, and don't act on them until it makes sense that you can achieve a positive goal. Learn to restrain yourself. Learning this process takes practice; it is not magic.

The essential problem with this concept is that people are human and we can often react automatically based on our feelings. Also, adversity can come in the form of withdrawal. Withdrawing love, care, or promises can lead an individual into worrisome circumstances.

In another example, the parents of a young married, expectant couple offered to give a large financial gift when their first grandchild was born. The young couple, James and Patty, were delighted, and they placed deposits on a crib and furniture with this promise.

Well, trouble came just like it does in everyone's life sooner or later and sometimes it can be caused by one's own family. James, in his early thirties, lost his job for no apparent reason.

The parents told them this was an opportunity to really help the young couple to grow, and they withdrew the promise of the money. They told the young couple they wouldn't appreciate this withdrawal of money until much later in life. The parents explained that when they were first married, financial hardship assisted them to become millionaires after the great depression.

They felt their children needed to fight through the monetary struggle and learn from it. The parents were reliving their past through their children—not a correct behavior.

Patty asked if I thought this concept would help them mature. I said, "No, it will not. The world is filled with strangers who will give you enough hardship, and you don't need to get the extra experience from your own family."

Feeling very discouraged, Patty asked why the in-laws acted in such an uncaring fashion.

I explained, "Sometimes parents want to communicate how they felt during tragic events in their lives. If they explained their struggle during the depression, you and your husband could only

31

intellectually understand it. You couldn't have known how it really felt living without monetary means unless your in-laws somehow demonstrated the same situation with you and James.

Intentionally and unintentionally these parents were repeating the story of their lives with their own children and causing trouble. I agreed with my client that it was a terrible situation to re-enact, especially since a child was on the way. I added, "This behavior is more common and widespread than one can imagine."

Patty asked what she could do about it. I thought about the story of King Solomon who threatened to cut a baby in half to determine which was the real mother. One mother shielded the baby from the sword and gave the baby to the other woman. Solomon knew that the real mother would give up her own child rather than sacrifice it. Sometimes it helps to create a situation for people to sacrifice as long as there is a positive goal.

I asked my client, "Are you willing to set up a risky situation for yourself, your husband and your in-laws by following my example?" She questioned what I had in mind.

I suggested Patty tell her husband to inform his parents if they wanted to ever see their grandchild, it would now require double the amount of the monetary gift. I explained, "His parents must have felt worthless during their monetary struggle, but they need to learn not to pass these unhealthy feelings on to others. Also, they need to understand that money isn't more important than family."

32

I explained. "If this intervention works, it will help the parents learn an emotional lesson about the importance of family."

My client went from feeling helpless and discouraged to possibly hopeful. She proposed the idea to her husband, but he refused to suggest this idea to his parents. Patty believed her husband was feeling too guilty because he assumed it was his parents' money, and they could do whatever they wanted with it. Patty was *fit to be tied*, and circumstances were at a standstill for the money.

The one aspect about life is that nothing stays the same for long; everything changes sooner or later. The idea is to be patient and wait for a possible lead into the situation to promote the desired change.

Months went by without any change in the situation, and James was still unemployed. Patty told me she felt something was going on with her husband's inability to obtain employment. She thought his lack of skill was related to his past.

During therapy, Patty talked about her husband's history, and reported that James had withdrawn from college many years previously when he needed only four more credits to graduate. She asked me to give him an appointment to try to help him obtain employment. I met James, who didn't have a clue as to why he wasn't employed.

Often it is difficult to look at ourselves and see the major themes in our Life Story, which can be obvious to others. James thought he was in an unlucky phase of his life.

I mentioned to him, "People make their own luck and we do have free will." At this point in time,

James did not realize that he was reliving a past history from his youth.

He explained, "I was up for a managerial position in a major company. I was literally the ninety-eighth person out of a hundred people to be interviewed. The interviewer informed me if the next two candidates were not better than me, I was going to get the position. I told the interviewer if I didn't get the job, I would understand and it would be okay."

In my opinion, this was a negative suggestion to give to the interviewer. I asked James why he made this comment. He replied, "I wanted to show the interviewer I was a nice guy." He wasn't offered the position.

There it was; his wife was right. James' past was holding him back from moving forward. He couldn't see he was repeating his Life Story with the withdrawal theme. He withdrew from college just at the point when he could have graduated. His parents had withdrawn their promise of money just at the point when it would have been very helpful. He created an environment with the interviewer which gave the interviewer the opportunity to withdraw his forthcoming job offer.

In this session, James realized if he had kept his mouth closed, he probably would have received the job. He believed he was stupid for speaking up.

I explained, "It has nothing to do with being unintelligent. It is simply a familiar behavior pattern to you. You are unconsciously re-enacting a theme from your life."

I realized this topic was instilled in him by his parents who trained him to accept withdrawn promises from them all of his life. I asked if he remembered any other times his parents withdrew pledges. He said, "There were quite a few times."

Once again I said to myself, *There it is.* He encouraged the interviewer to act like his parents. I reported this fact to him, and he was amazed he hadn't seen this for himself.

I explained, "Many times people can't see their own life Themes. It has nothing to do with one's academic intelligence—it has to do with Emotional Intelligence."

On his next job interview, James managed to obtain the position. Furthermore, seeing the positive outcome, he decided to follow the plan I suggested in regard to his parents.

He told them to re-offer the monetary gift or they could not see the grandchild. The parents held out until a week before the baby was born. They gave a check for twice the amount and this apparently did help the young couple financially and emotionally to feel appreciated.

The grandparents even admitted to the young couple that it was a good idea for them to be put into this situation to choose between money and family. "Helping the family gave us great satisfaction."

I was certainly glad that my intervention helped the whole family move forward. It was a bumpy and risky ride but the outcome was successful. It was particularly rewarding to apply my personal experience to help another family feel cared for. The theme of early withdrawal of promises can be obvious to an outsider, such as me, but not to the person going through it.

Instilling emotions in another person is quite common. Some people are able to verbalize these emotions to another about a terrible event, but the listeners might not actually perceive all the sensations related to this occurrence. To explain this idea further, another client related a relevant experience to me.

ELSA'S LIFE THEME OF BEING CAUGHT IN THE LIFE STORY OF HER PARENTS

Elsa was a New York City high school teacher in her early fifties. Her family and her husband's family were survivors of the Holocaust. The survivors talked at length about this topic of great significance but the listeners couldn't truly feel the emotions that were described.

Over the years, she heard tragic stories and could only intellectually sympathize with the death of six million people. When she heard these events, it sounded like a history lesson.

On a trip to Europe, Elsa visited some of the concentration camps. The tour group followed the same route as a group of people had faced before they were executed. She saw shoes and hair piled from the floor to the ceiling in one of the buildings. The number of the people who were murdered started to arouse feelings of sadness and anger in her.

Elsa explained to me that she now emotionally realized how it must have felt for those people to go through the horrible nightmare. This experience gave her a base line to empathize with what her relatives had gone through. She shared, "I have grown to know how others were affected by these events, and how these events continue to influence my parents' life."

Elsa's parents had been over-protective through her entire life. For example, when she left their house, her parents asked her to telephone home so that they knew she arrived home safely. Now she understood their fear about her safety.

> *Happiness is a balance between love, work,*
> *and play. Until this balance is achieved,*
> *you need to be relatively comfortable.*

Figure out what makes you angry and find ways to avoid it. Content individuals become sad less frequently and the feelings do not last long because these people have the ability to redirect themselves into pleasurable activities.

Every day should be a new chapter in the book of your life. You must move forward into new directions to grow. My clients were able to move on—some moved into new experiences faster than others but all of them made the effort. I have come to the realization that if more people are able to feel their emotions and understand them, the healthier they will be.

Understanding The Past

Your common sense has the ability to push you forward but your emotional past filled with unresolved trouble has the ability to push you back. One of my clients suffered from this situation. Her goal in therapy was to obtain a balanced life.

MS. M's LIFE STORY OF ABUSE
AND THEME OF RUNNING AWAY

Ms. M was in her mid-thirties, a very attractive woman who was quite accomplished in her career.

On the outside it appeared to others that she was living the *American Dream*. Yet, my client felt she was constantly living in a nightmare. At night, her dreams were filled with scenarios of people chasing her and in the morning, she felt exhausted. She did not know who was chasing her or why she was running.

Ms. M has an interesting Life Story. She felt too frightened to enter into matrimony. She had a lot of difficulty taking responsibility for her actions. She never completely understood why she terminated relationships.

She said, "I know marriage isn't perfect and couples have to work at a successful union, but I ran away from the commitment. Help me to complete my life. I want to marry and I want to have at least one child."

Her life consisted with fleeting periods of happiness, and I knew her trouble related to her Life Story. Most of Ms. M's sessions consisted of stories about her friends and about her work associates which did not give a clue why she was running in her dreams.

After many sessions, she became comfortable with me. Transference occurred and she saw me as the caring father that she never had. (Transference occurs when a person transfers feelings of one person—whether he wishes to or not—onto another person). This happens to everyone, not only in therapy.

She stated that I would have protected her from her mother's rage. One day she related a story which told me where her difficulties arose.

Ms. M described a memory that came to her, "When I was eight-years old, I realized I could escape from my mother's brutal wrath depending upon which room in the apartment was closer, the bathroom or the kitchen. If I didn't escape, it meant her 5 ft. 9 inch tall and 165-lb. body entrapped me. I was hit or beaten by whatever object was readily available. This ranged from a wooden hanger, a leather belt, a wet dishcloth, or just her bare hands.

"Running into the bathroom was the safest route because it had a lock on the door. It was, however, an uncomfortable room especially during the winter when the tile floor was cold. Another route for me was the kitchen. The kitchen's advantage over the bathroom was there was a linoleum floor that was warmer than the ceramic tile floor. In the kitchen, I was able to stretch out and sleep except for an occasional cockroach tickling my nose with its feelers.

"There was one problem; the kitchen door had no lock. I learned that I could improvise a locked door by taking some rope from an adjacent cabinet and very quickly connecting the doorknob of a large cabinet to a nearby steam pipe. Thus, I made a closed-in area for protection.

"My mother knew where I kept the rope, and she never took it away. Apparently she enjoyed the game of chase and torture. Sometimes I made it to safety and sometimes I couldn't. When I couldn't make it to safety, she hit me, and my crying in pain never seemed to stop her. She stopped when she became tired."

Ms. M stated that when her mother was in this mood, her father walked out of the apartment. There was no one to save her.

At this point, Ms. M was sobbing. She continued, "When my mother's rage calmed down, she would usually tell me that I had 'learned my lesson,' and that I could come into the living room to watch television.

"I never understood what she wanted me to learn. I knew enough not to ask, with the risk of getting her angry again. At an early age, I didn't realize my mother had a unique capacity for cruelty, and it was difficult for me to understand how she used me for her own amusement. It was her version of the game of cat and mouse. She was the cat and I was the mouse who was tortured. I guess her desire to control me and to keep me afraid was her way to keep me close to her."

When Ms. M understood where her trouble began, she realized she had the strength to move in a better direction. She understood that everyone has some sort of trouble in life, and our past is never truly behind us. These memories drift back into our life, especially the bottled up anger from the past and the inability to confront the conflict.

It wasn't the emotions themselves that created problems for Ms. M, but it was her inability to be connected with them. Before this session, she was in a state of repression involving a loss of memory for certain incidents, especially traumatic, painful ones.

40

Ms. M had the ability to suppress her emotions over the years, and this suppression made her feelings clouded and distorted. No matter how much she protested that she had these memories, they remained hidden in her mind. If she did not verbalize them and understand them, they had the ability to influence her behavior and make trouble.

Ms. M wanted to be in control of her destiny but when she became engaged, she feared she was placing herself in a situation similar to that as a child—being reliant on others for her well-being and happiness. She felt scared of entrapment because she believed her future husband could have a personality similar to her mother who also stated that she loved her.

I explained that whatever had gone wrong in her life, whatever misconceptions or mistakes she made, it is possible to move ahead and find satisfaction and comfort in her life.

During that session and others, she realized that in order to move forward, one has to deal with the past and rid ourselves from the problem which caused the trouble. No one can go back to one's past to reverse what has happened. She knew that she gained great wisdom from expressing this experience.

In retrospect, Ms. M's inability to see her true childhood and her poor judgment in believing that her mother was capable of loving and caring for her, caused hardships throughout her life. She learned that just because she felt something was going to happen, it didn't necessarily mean it would occur.

Through the process of our sessions, Ms. M knew she survived a horrible childhood with an abusive mother. She realized she could find a loving, life-long companion without repeating this ill-treated scenario.

41

She reported that the feeling of hopelessness did not creep into her mind as often. The recognition that she was a strong individual who has gotten through past trouble was the source of hope for her.

Ms. M married successfully and had two children. She thanked me for helping her discover the negative Themes in her life and to create a positive environment.

Everyone's life reflects a struggle for survival. It is how you respond to adversity that defines you as a person. Sometimes it is hard to perceive that out of bad times there can be good outcomes to change your outlook. It is a learning lesson. Your Life Story helps to define you; however, you have the ability to change for the better.

> *The secret lies in knowing that you have choices about how you look at external events, how you feel about them, how you attribute meaning to them, and how you react to them emotionally.*

The Power of Money

One of the most valuable self-evaluations we can do is to look at the attitudes that we inherited or absorbed from our parents or adults around us. A client's former life style—related to his parents' attitude towards spending money—made him emotionally sick.

THOMAS' LIFE STORY OF ABSORBING BELIEFS
AND FEAR FROM PARENTS

Thomas was a recent college graduate who had trouble relating to his friends when they went out socially. He really didn't want to split the check. Thomas stated emphatically that individual checks should be given. He felt it was unfair to pay for some else's expensive dinner when he was eating the day's special.

I realized his problems related to his Life Story. Old ghosts of his Life Story became a voyage into discovering his *true self*. His discovery was a bumpy trip to get where he is today. Looking back, his parents appeared to love...and even worship... money over their own children. It is strange how money and feelings are so often intertwined in relationships. It is even more interesting how money can be (a) utilized to hurt other people's feelings and (b) the power to control individuals.

Thomas related a story about his Bar Mitzvah. According to Jewish law, Jewish children who reach the age of maturity of 13 years become responsible for their actions. At this point in life, a boy has a traditional ceremony called a Bar Mitzvah. After this age, boys

43

are privileged to participate in all areas of Jewish community life and bear responsibility for Jewish ritual law, tradition and ethics.

After his Bar Mitzvah ceremony, Thomas' parents had a party to celebrate the event. His mother had purchased a suit from Alexander's Department Store. After the party, she reattached the price tickets to his new blue suit and returned it to the store.

My client wanted the suit to be his gift, but his mother said, "You cannot keep the suit because you do not need it."

To further understand his desire for the suit, his parents rarely bought him clothes; thus his longing was based on his previous history. He always wore his uncle's *hand-me downs*. His uncle was at least thirty-years older than Thomas and his worn clothes were neither in his size nor his taste. Thomas' parents told him he was still growing and using their money to buy clothes would be wasteful.

Thomas asked his father, "How much money are you placing in my savings account for college?"

The father calmly responded, "You will get nothing." His father was planning to take the proceeds to pay himself back for what he laid out for the party. Traditionally monetary gifts are usually given for future education.

His parents made it an elaborate occasion that was totally inappropriate for that era of time. His mother bought a stylish business suit for the temple services and a lovely cocktail dress for the party. Both outfits had matching accessories. His father bought a new blue suit, new black shoes, new tie and shirt.

It appeared to Thomas that it was important for his parents to put on a show for others. His parents' articles of clothes were not returned to the stores.

His sister who had a full-time job bought a dress that she kept because she bought it with her own money.

I taught Thomas that the true character of a person can best be seen not in the public eye but what the person does in private. His parents wanted others to see them as caring and loving parents. This was essentially how he was raised—under a cloud of misrepresentation.

He got what they thought he needed, not necessarily what Thomas wanted. When this happens, it is not unusual for a person to feel not cared for. It was hard for him to acknowledge the fact that his family did not value him; they valued money.

As my client related, both of his parents were employed and they didn't need the money to pay for the party. Also, they could have afforded to buy the first new suit he ever had, or they could have placed some of the monetary gifts into a college account.

When he reached college age, Thomas had to take out loans for school and work part-time for his personal expenses. His parents did not help. When he was an adult, his parents died. Upon their death, they left him and his sister nothing. He realized, in therapy, that money did not make anyone in his family happy or cared for; however, using this money in his youth would have been emotionally beneficial to him.

Many times my client tried to rationalize his mother's and father's behavior towards his Bar Mitzvah. He thought it might have related to their own childhood of growing up with immigrant parents who had very little money.

He used convincing reasons to justify their conduct so as to avoid recognizing their true underlying motive that was unacceptable to him; he continued to

45

make excuses for his parents' behavior. It was extremely difficult for him to face the fact that his parents did not care for him.

His mother repeated to him many times that as a young woman living in her parents' home, she had to give her paycheck to her father. He wondered, *Is she repeating the same pattern with me and inducing similar reactions of not feeling cared for?*

His mother had a way of making him believe he owed her something which was missing in her own childhood. She constantly told him that she *gave her life on a silver platter* to him, and he was a lucky child. Yet he never felt any sort of loving concern on his mother's part.

Thomas tried to make his mother happy and it was not an easy task because she remained unsatisfied with whatever he did for her. Listening to my client describe his childhood, I wondered who the adult was and who the child was in this relationship.

During his childhood, the issue of the importance of money came about again with money winning over his well-being. He related another story.

Thomas played basketball in junior high school. In practice, he jumped up and landed with his leg at an awkward angle, and heard something click. Being unsure what happened, he managed to walk home. While walking home, his leg started to throb with pain.

At home he pleaded with his mother that his leg might be broken and he needed to see a doctor. His mother did not get his leg X-rayed until the third day. Thomas had a hairline fracture and a cast was applied. Instead of purchasing a wooden cane to help him with his mobility, his mother borrowed a wooden cane from a neighbor which was too short for him to get around comfortably.

Recuperating from his injury, Thomas was lying on the couch and sensed from his mother's extremely loud noises around the apartment that she was in one of her cruel moods. She voiced, "I have to take care of you and I do not feel like it."

After living many years with his mother's personality, it gave my client the ability to think critically and analyze information quickly in order to react to her cruel disposition. When his mother went to grab the cane so did he; they fought for possession and he won.

For the first time in his life, Thomas was so exasperated by the incident, he went on the offensive. With all his strength, he swung the cane at his mother. Fortunately, she jumped out of the way. The cane hit the adjacent wall, and the cane cracked in half.

After this incident, he said, "My mother was very cautious about ever trying to hit me again."

He, too, was careful, and he didn't want to push his luck by asking his mother about the situation of having his leg fixed because she might demonstrate one of her sudden rages.

A few days after this incident, he asked his mother, "Why didn't you take me to the doctor earlier?" She stated, "I didn't want to spend the money."

Remembering this incident again gave him the feeling he was an unwanted child who was a burden upon his family. My client asked me questions, such as: "Was my mother re-enacting her Life Story over money through me? Why weren't her siblings acting in a similar pattern with their families? Why was my mother the only violent one in her family?"

As a child, she made Thomas feel guilty that she had to take responsibility for him, so he made excuses for her behavior. He did not want to face the fact that

47

she was not concerned over his well-being. Throughout his childhood, my client had the unique ability to ward off her unacceptable conduct with excuses, but he wasn't able to erase her bad behavior from his unconscious mind, which lasted throughout his adulthood.

Thomas recognized his upbringing was causing his trouble. He had to face the cause, accept it without excuses, understand it, and move away from it into positive behavior.

Gradually my client had to understand that the concept of friendship and caring is more important than money. With my guidance, he learned not to act on his feelings towards money but to act on what he wanted out of life.

One of his goals was having a non-stressful life filled with people who cared about him. Thomas' life was a constant battle with his unconscious pattern of association with selfish people. Overcoming the unrest his parents presented to him, he is now beginning to enjoy true friendships, and able to spend money without feeling he doesn't deserve the pleasure. He is beginning to have a more fulfilled life as a worthwhile individual.

When you are faced with inner trouble, this turmoil prevents you from expressing your full range of capabilities and prevents you from enjoying your time to the utmost. Learning to understand this turmoil is emotionally beneficial to your growth. Your troubles could be a productive way to understand your life's direction. These dilemmas demonstrate where your anger and regrets are coming from. It is important to acknowledge these negative energies; then you have the power to re-organize your life accordingly. A positive attitude in life will get results as long as it is in conjunction with positive action.

Set Backs to Success

No one likes to relive failures. It is tempting to hide unpleasant memories or even to pretend they never happened. Failure is a way to learn and to grow as a person.

Lessons in life are necessary because through adversity one grows and progresses.

BRIAN'S LIFE STORY OF PROTECTING HIS MOTHER
AND THEME OF NOT FEELING WORTHY OF ATTENTION

A well-built gentleman in his forties sought out counseling with me. He was having personal dilemmas, and he felt his life had always been difficult. His troubles were hard to bear and he constantly felt like a failure. Being uncomfortable in this negative state, Brian sought out therapy.

He stated that he had been having many setbacks against achieving any success in life. Brian related a story from his youth.

When he was eighteen-years old, Brian received a full-paid scholarship to play basketball at a NCAA Division I (top category for athletic competition) school in New Mexico. He was really happy and excited with his new venture.

Looking back at his full-paid scholarship, it appeared his immediate family was jealous of his good luck. Brian realized his mother felt he was abandoning her—after all she felt she was a good mother and a child of hers should not leave her.

The morning he was going to his new school, Brian woke up early; he took two suitcases to the subway and arrived at JFK Airport alone. His family never said goodbye or had any celebration.

Previously his mother had emphasized, "Call home every Sunday at three o'clock." Being an inconsistent personality, she also said, "I hope the plane crashes for you leaving me. Otherwise, make sure you flunk out of school so you can come home."

Brian expressed that he was glad to leave home and wouldn't have to listen to his parents' arguments and negativity towards him.

Brian shared that another fellow student from his high school was taking the same plane out of JFK Airport to go to Arizona. This young man later became a famous NBA player.

What impressed my client was the fact that this athlete's entire family came to the airport to support his new venture and they even bought him a present. They told him that they were going to miss him and wished him good fortune. His family gave him hugs and kisses.

This was a great contrast to Brian's family who showed no interest.

The essential part of this story is that Brian didn't feel worthy of attention...so how could he become successful? Not feeling any emotion placed him in a mental state of not trying his all or his best.

In New Mexico, Brian walked through practice and through the games in a manner similar to sleep walking. He was not totally there; part of him was thinking about his dysfunctional life, and he was not focused.

Even as his mother insisted that he call on Sundays, it was a way of controlling him. Again she confused him by stating her love which was not in accordance with her actions.

> *Control isn't a form of caring;*
> *it is a form of manipulation.*

Brian told me that the phone calls home consisted of complex human communication which was all one-sided. His mother made him feel he caused her unhappiness with his father. She was never concerned about his progress in college.

After those conversations, he felt conflicted with his role in the family. He questioned himself, *What am I—a son or a mediator between my parents? What can I do to help her from New Mexico?*

Facing conflicting forces in his personal life made him unable to direct his attention to his basketball career, and the negative forces demonstrated by his mother made him prone to become involved in another failure.

From my experience, the amount of success or failure a person encounters in life is directly related to how much he felt affection from others in growing up. Brian's colleague from high school felt admiration because his family demonstrated it, and he became an accomplished basketball player.

The story of my client's life repeated itself. The college he attended had a coach who said he was going to develop his playing talents yet he did not follow through. The coach spent all of his time with more advanced players, and Brian was on his own again. The feeling of abandonment overcame him. It was similar to his family's behavior. The coach gave him a false impression that he was going to nurture him.

Listening and believing in false words became a problem for Brian most of his life. It became a struggle to analyze people who were capable of telling lies.

During the basketball season, Brian was injured in practice. Indirectly he was being beaten again emotionally. He had been fooled by the coach's words that he would help him. This incident exacerbated his negative feelings about whether he was ever going to be successful in life.

Basketball had been so much a part of his future plans, but with the injury he was not quite sure what to do with his life. His early failures took a big toll out of any joy he could envision for his life.

At the end of Brian's freshman year, his basketball scholarship wasn't renewed. Feeling discouraged, he transferred back to a school in the east.

At home, his father stated, "I am disappointed in you because I was counting on the fact you would become a basketball star and earn a high income. I was hoping your income would support me in my old age."

This statement came from a man who never encouraged him, never gave him any kind words, or never attended any of his high school games. His father was placing Brian in the position of being his parent and supporting him. This was a big role for a teenager to comprehend.

He stopped pursuing basketball and graduated college with a major in history. Teaching appeared to be a good option for him to pursue. Not surprisingly, this is what his mother had wanted him to do—and she again was in control.

Nothing came easy for Brian, and he felt like a failure by becoming a history teacher. Eventually he moved on to a higher rank in the Board of Education which gave him a feeling of success.

The money he earned gave him the opportunity to explore different ways of enjoying life. Some summers he worked and other summers he travelled abroad. He saw how others lived and perceived life which opened his eyes to happiness and contentment. In time, he broke his emotional ties with his parents and kept them at arm's length until their deaths.

> *The greatest risk from failure is not failure itself,*
> *but that it may make you think that you are a*
> *loser—if you allow yourself to believe it.*

You could be a successful person who merely had a bad moment—this was the lesson that Brian was learning from therapy. He became a winner in life. You can also be a winner by analyzing your situation and knowing that you have the ability to achieve success.

Creating Reality

We create our own reality by the choices we make. Many of our choices are fueled by our memories and experiences...in other words, the Story of our Life.

> *By remembering misfortunes and the confusions that it brought to your mind, you can overcome another's power to manipulate you*

Always keep in mind that the common denominator in every relationship is you. You must believe you can change your behavior for the better to become a person who has successful relationships with others. Even if, initially, you don't believe it, work at it anyway; it will happen.

PAUL'S THEME OF CONTROL TO AVOID REPEATING HIS PARENTS' BEHAVIOR

A male client in his early twenties who was recently married came to me for therapy. He described his family structure as containing a mother who was the dominate figure over his father. It had caused a great deal of unhappiness within the family. Paul didn't want to repeat this behavior in his marriage, but recognized that it was becoming a difficult task to accomplish.

Paul commented that his mother often said, with a smile on her face, "I like to stir the pot." Looking back at her behavior he explained, "She enjoyed causing jealousy and trouble within the family; that was her entertainment." According to Paul, his mother had the ability to move people and circumstances to her advantage.

He married a girl who came from a different background. Her family was the positive image family that one might watch on a television sitcom. It was the family my client longed for; it was a place where he could find comfort and peace. There was a feeling of safety, structure and stability.

Home is the ultimate place where you should receive your value as a person, and hers was such a home—an atmosphere filled with music, laughter, and conversation.

One might say my client had the perfect home life, but he started trouble by creating a negative environment which was familiar to him. Not realizing what he was doing, he was sabotaging his relationship.

> *You can manage your actions*
> *if you understand the Story of your Life.*

Part of his confusion was Paul's inability to accept a tenderhearted wife and her family. He created constant friction with his wife because his parents always fought over everything no matter how small or insignificant. Unfortunately, he was re-living his past childhood experiences with his wife.

An example of this friction could be summed up in the following story. His wife wanted to buy a vacuum cleaner for their apartment. She knew exactly what she wanted; she wanted a Hoover just like her mother's vacuum.

On the other hand, my client had a desire to control the situation. He asked a salesman in the store his opinion on different vacuum cleaners. The salesman stated that the best vacuum cleaner was Eureka, and he showed the young couple *Consumer Reports* which clearly rated Eureka as number one and Hoover as number three.

In my client's opinion, it was settled; Eureka was the best vacuum cleaner. His wife stated again that she wanted a Hoover, but he insisted she was wrong on her choice and she was not being logical. Following his mother's pattern of behavior, he was trying to be in control and determining what someone else wanted. He was so insistent, his wife ran crying out of the store into a busy intersection, almost getting hit by a car. This situation troubled him.

The instability from his own family had carried over into his adulthood. He was *beside himself* and didn't know what to do.

That week he discussed the whole story with me, and he was convinced I would see it his way. I understood his way of viewing the situation but also saw his wife's way of thinking.

I explained to him the best vacuum cleaner for his wife was the Hoover because that was what she needed emotionally. Her mother had one and she liked it. It had nothing to do with logic. His wife emotionally felt cared for, and she believed her mother would not give her bad advice.

After that session he told his wife that they should get the Hoover and she thanked him. She never reprimanded him for acting in a dominant way. My client realized he was causing trouble similar to his mother who said, "I like to stir the pot." Paul had trouble with others because he liked being the dominant person in every situation.

He became aware of how much his past affected his daily behavior, and he had to avoid unreasonable actions and making mistakes in judgment.

Paul realized he had repeated what I call a Theme in his Life's Story. He was being the architect of his own destiny in not caring what his wife wanted— he was repeating the example provided by his parents. It seemed he couldn't be in a close personal situation for a long time without making trouble. His present day dilemma was a reaction to his Life Story.

After he understood where the trouble started, he had the ability to confront the unrest and redefine it into more positive behavior. Paul learned not to automatically act on his feelings. He started to act on what made sense in order to have a happy outcome. Today he is content in letting others make decisions.

On the other hand, my client's wife, Alice, acted in a way that repeated her Life Story in the following episode.

THE INTERMINGLING OF ALICE'S LIFE STORY
WITH HER MOTHER'S

Paul's wife, Alice, had difficulty rising above the story of her life with her mother. Her mother was legally deaf and growing up was challenging because her mother didn't hear any of her requests.

As a young pre-school child, she asked her mother for a cookie and her mother gave her a pretzel. Instead of stating her request again, she remembers walking away from her mother without a pretzel or a cookie because she knew her mother couldn't hear.

58

As a youngster, she realized repeating herself would not solve the problem. Later on, she learned that if she moved the kitchen chair to the cabinet, she could stand on the chair, get herself upon the counter, and open the cabinet to get the snack she wanted. Alice learned at an early age to be self-reliant.

She must have felt helpless with her mother at various times in a similar way that she felt with her husband. Alice's contribution was that she operated in a way that Paul couldn't hear her – she ran away.

So, the story of a person's life intermingles in relationships. You need to understand and emerge from it. Sometimes it is not so easy to see the event at the time, but if you look back you can learn from it. You may recognize something that you couldn't have seen at the time.

> *Take a step back and think about what is happening. Try to refrain from acting on your emotions. There is a connection between your present circumstances and your Life Story.*

Looking back on these episodes has taught me a great deal in relationships. The overall emotions of love can be summed up as generosity toward your partner.

> *Marriage is not a game in which you keep score of who wins and who loses arguments.*

A partnership needs an attitude of being on the same side; we are allies, not adversaries trying to gain power over the other. With this attitude, it will help you focus on the good aspects of your relationship. It will let you diminish the time and energy spent on the negative aspects of your association.

It is amazing how problems in a relationship disappear when one focuses on acceptance, thoughtfulness, and tolerance. As mentioned, you can feel disappointed or angry inside, but you should not act upon these emotions. You can choose to behave in a good-natured way towards your partner and you will create harmony and connection.

> *You cannot stop your feelings,*
> *but you have a choice in the way you act.*

The general public often has a misconception of love in a relationship. Society tends to think of carefree images of romantic music, candy and flowers. What of love through the hard times and the stresses which occur in a marriage?

> *The development, maintenance, and willingness to work*
> *jointly on a relationship is important to its success. The*
> *idea is to keep helping each other, especially when life gets*
> *difficult and when you might not feel the warmth.*

Positive emotions will usually return if the partners stick to their compassionate goals and benefits accrue to both parties when there is a strong bond.

Love is a selfless action of giving help to your partner without being asked or hoping he will return the deed. Love isn't a barter system; the warm smile of your loved one can be enough reward to the giver.

Studies have shown people in a caring situation live longer and are happier than those who don't. When people believe they are in a good relationship, great things can happen to them. They feel they are empowered and grow emotionally.

Relationships are severe tests of emotional strength for people, and the early upbringing of an individual comes into motion during these strenuous times. How you associate with your partner has to do with your Life Story.

Helping Each Other

If one person helps another, the other will follow by helping the first one when it is needed. A philosopher once stated that all good work is done little by little, the way that ants work. Just like ants, it is a gradual process all through one's lifetime. Success doesn't come overnight.

CATHERINE'S LIFE STORY OF INDEPENDENCE
AND THEME OF "I HAVE TO DO IT ALL MYSELF"

Catherine was an attractive young teacher in her early twenties. Her undergraduate student teaching experience did not prepare her for classes in a junior high school in Brooklyn, NY. The students were from low-income families where the students often struggled with one parent or a grandmother raising them.

Through therapy, Catherine realized individuals have a great hand in forming their destiny. Teaching students in the seventh and eighth age bracket is difficult because they are not children and they are not adults. They are young teenagers.

For the first time in the school system students were moving individually from one classroom to another, giving them freedom they never before had. Thus, they were experimenting with their ability to grow up, to overpower adult figures, and to discover their limitations.

On Sunday nights, Catherine shared that she emotionally suffered with worry about how to handle misbehaving students in the afternoon classes. Of course, anxiety in anticipation of one's job is obviously not limited to teachers.

62

I wanted to aid my client in her dilemma. I asked if there was anything I could do to help. She responded with certainty, "Nothing."

It took me a while to realize she was re-enacting her Life Story into the teaching dilemma and also into therapy.

Catherine was raised by a mother who was hard of hearing, and she was an only child. For this reason, my client had poor communication skills in asking for assistance.

As a result of her upbringing, she essentially had to figure out things on her own. As a child, she knew she couldn't ask for advice because her mother couldn't hear her.

In therapy, Catherine had a tendency to speak loudly and was usually not aware of it. I surmised the reason she spoke loudly was because she assumed the listener didn't hear her, and she wanted to be heard. I learned that my client had very little verbal direction from her mother and thought to myself, *She might not want advice from me unless she asks for it.*

Many times this happens in therapy and in life where people do not ask for support. It is as if they think others should know what they want without having to say anything.

> *If you think others know what you want,*
> *you are usually mistaken.*

One day Catherine reported that she had a rough Friday afternoon teaching. I asked if she wanted me to give any suggestions in handling the behavior problem.

63

She responded, "No, I will have to figure it out on my own."

There is a formula to help someone in a relationship as long as you understand the story of his life. Catherine did not want advice at this point; she just wanted to vent her emotions, and the correct skill is to become a good listener. Many times the classroom experiences were so painful and upsetting she suppressed her emotions; therefore, her feelings were not clear to her.

When she became willing to share her school day, it freed her from inner emotional turmoil. Through this process of verbalization, she was able to discuss her problem, and her channel for discussion opened up.

I told Catherine a story about one of my other clients who was an experienced teacher. Mr. Johnson would visit parents on Saturday mornings in the housing projects. Word went around among the students about his actions, which were viewed by all as caring and positive. The parents actually welcomed his house calls, and the teacher's goal was for parents to know what was going on with their children in school. Most of the parents offered Mr. Johnson breakfast or a cup of coffee. I explained to Catherine that Mr. Johnson had few behavior problems in class.

The following week, Catherine was distressed about her worst class. I certainly did not expect her to make house calls.

I said, "I wonder what would happen if a teacher phoned the student's home early Saturday morning, introduce herself to the parents, and expressed that she needed their aid to better understand their child. In other words, ask the parents for their help."

I did not tell her to do something; I just made a suggestion. In other words, I put the idea in front of her to see if she wanted to use it. She stated that the parent might be angry with the teacher calling, especially early on a Saturday morning.

I agreed with her, only if the teacher approached the parent the way many teachers do...by just complaining. In that case, it would be a problem.

Often, teachers start off conversations with parents on a negative note. These conversations between teachers and parents consist of complaints on the child's behavior, inability to do homework assignments, and poor test scores. Most parents who receive similar calls and reports get turned off immediately and do not listen.

I continued, "I wonder what would happen if the teacher phoned and made the parent an ally. What if the teacher expressed the idea she was asking the parent for assistance in understanding what was preventing the child from being more successful in school?"

Questioning is a process which involves requests for more information as to the nature of the problem. I suggested getting into a discussion with the parent.

I stressed the phrase "preventing success" is important because it gives one the idea that an outside force is causing the problem, and it isn't critical of the child or the parent. The phone call would make the parent aware of what his child is doing in school, and it could help the parent to fix or assist in the situation. Some parents might need a few phone calls.

65

There could be difficulties in communicating thoughts between both parties but follow-up calls could eliminate this difficulty. These phone calls might give the parent and child a feeling that the teacher is a positive element in the school system.

My client had no response to this conversation at that time; she just listened.

Catherine decided to make some phone calls the following Saturday morning after a rough afternoon with her students.

She told me that at first the parents seemed taken by surprise until she asked for their help. She said, "Eventually the conversations worked very well." Within the month, all her classes were cooperative and doing the class work.

An interesting experience arose from this method of handling misbehaving students. One time Catherine was absent and the substitute teacher, who was supposed to cover her classes, was assigned to another teacher's room by mistake. Her classes were so cooperative and quiet the assistant principal on her floor didn't know of this error…that there was no teacher in the room.

For the first four periods of the school day, Catherine's students came into the classroom and worked independently from the assignments in their folders. Only after the assistant principal came into the room to check on the substitute teacher and class, did he realize that no teacher was in attendance and the students were quietly working. The assistant principal was impressed with the performance of this young teacher's ability to guide the students into good behavior.

I was able to help my client by creating an environment to reverse the troubled, non-hearing section of the Story of her Life. After this experience, she sought out my opinion on various issues which helped her students' performance. Her students and their parents felt someone was concerned about them as individuals. It became a win-win situation for all concerned.

I give similar advice to my clients who are teachers and parents—they benefit from talking in a positive manner to others. This advice is especially handy to teachers when the parent is being negative towards them.

On the other hand, I also recommend to parents that they not criticize their children's teachers but make them allies. Ask them for aid to assist their child and ask for the teacher's opinion as to what is preventing their child from being successful in school. This may encourage a teacher to become more positive towards the student.

The task is to search out a common ground between both parties' perception of what is needed to achieve the goal.

Negative feelings can block the advancement of teacher-student relationships and cause trouble for all. Remember, teachers and parents must work as a unit to get results.

Revisiting One's Past

There are two important concepts which are vital to a person's well-being: love and trust from others. An uncompassionate parent can detract from the parent-child bond and make the childhood fragmented. When the child doesn't have warm feelings in his home, he becomes confused and feels helpless and hopeless in life.

When a child acknowledges his parents' affection, he knows his parents are invested in his well-being. Knowing this fact, the child can rely on consistently caring responses whether he did well or poorly in any endeavor; the feeling of security in having loving parents is reinforced. Over time consistently positive responses add up, representing the healthy connection between parents and children.

MASON'S LIFE STORY WITH DESTRUCTIVE PARENTS AND CREATING A NEW SELF IMAGE

In the early 1970's a young male gym teacher who was on his first assignment for the New York City Board of Education came into my office. His job was an awakening for him. He was raised by destructive, uncaring parents which he considered was normal behavior. He thought children in ghetto neighborhoods had parents with worse personality faults than his.

Mason discovered the truth about different parental behaviors through his new job. He had no idea of what life was like in a ghetto; he had a distorted picture that these pupils didn't have any type of family structure. Some people believe that children with one parent don't come from a caring home life. The fact is

68

that many of these single parents have the ability to demonstrate loving feelings which are important in a child's development.

This 25-year old client came from a family life which can be described as empty and sad; his early life experience lacked sympathetic responses from his parents. Also, his parents had limited impulse control and tolerance for children. As his students developed relationships with him, they revealed many things which were foreign in terms of his own childhood experience.

Through his students, Mason learned that most of their family members had the ability to identify with each other and trust one another. On the other hand, Mason's childhood was plagued with so many imperfections and interpersonal difficulties that anxiety arose in the structure and was detrimental to everyone's self-esteem.

Mason related, "My pupils want to learn, obtain skills and knowledge so that they can improve their standard of living." He described that their families protect the children by maintaining ties that are helpful; and there is a deep sense of commitment, obligation and responsibility to all.

When Mason was teaching a hygiene class about sex education this commitment issue arose. A student who was 13-years old with dark-black curly hair and large brown eyes mentioned his mother told him that if he tongue-kissed a girl, it would lead to pregnancy.

Mason realized that the student's mother was trying to shield her child from becoming an unwed father. She wanted him to finish school and become successful. The child believed his affectionate parent and never questioned her philosophy.

69

Since my client was the instructor, he felt that he had to tell him the truth. He also explained to the pupil that his loving mother was looking out for his future, and she wanted him to become accomplished in the world. The child's experience will, to a degree, determine the nature of an ideal distortion from his family because the child knows his family is caring and loving.

Mason also related a story which was a profound example of a mother's nurturing ability. It occurred in his gym class.

The class was split up into various teams to play basketball. It was quite warm in the gym so some of the students took off their shirts. During a supervised activity, a youngster developed an uncontrollable nosebleed.

Carlos was a popular 15-year-old male student of medium height and weight, who had a great smile. Mason performed in the manner dictated by his training. He put Carlos in a prostrate position, directed him to the pressure points on his palate which would staunch the flow of blood, and applied ice. The student's bleeding would not stop.

The teenager tried to explain to Mason that he had lost his religious cross; it had snapped from his neck during his energetic play.

Carlos emphasized, "My mother warned me I shouldn't lose my cross; I must keep it close to me at all times. If I lose it, my nose will start to bleed."

His nose did bleed uncontrollably because he trusted his mother's words. A fellow pupil was able to locate the gold cross on the floor, and miraculously the nosebleed stopped as precipitously as it had begun.

Two months later this youngster again lost his cross, and his nose began to bleed. Another gym teacher noticed Carlos's nose was bleeding and he proceeded to get an ice pack.

Mason blew his whistle and asked the class for help in finding the cross. It was found. This time no ice was applied to his nose, and the bleeding stopped as soon as the cross was placed around Carlos's neck.

Mason said to the student, "You must really believe and respect your mother to trust her." He responded

"My mother is my whole world and everything to me." You could definitely view the affection Carlos had for his mother. You could sense that his mother was a kind woman who valued her son, and was committed to care for him.

Trust is a confident reliance on the integrity and honesty of another. One must earn trust for another person to sense it.

This concept was interesting to my client because he worked in a school where most of the students lived below the poverty line and they had concerned mothers.

Giving love doesn't cost anyone money; it is freely given. Money is not the strongest aspect in life; it is love.

The two boys in these stories felt the devotion they received from their mothers; therefore, they trusted them. They knew their mothers were working in their best interests, and wouldn't hurt them physically or mentally.

Unfortunately it was hard for my client to relate to this concept of trust since it was denied to him as a youngster. Nevertheless, through these students he was able to indirectly experience the feelings of security that children should have.

In therapy, as my client was learning more about how to handle his issues from childhood, he also learned how to help others. Mason continued to relate stories to me about caring individuals and how children also can receive caring emotions from outsiders.

One of his larger Physical Education classes, with an enrollment of 70 students, consisted of a small group of destructive boys who suffered from aggressive behavior and negative attitudes.

A 13-year old, Michael, who was quite shy in the class had a severe stuttering problem, and he drew the attention and ridicule of some of his peers. It seemed his disorder was accentuated whenever he addressed an authority figure.

If my client contacted him in the course of a lesson that required him to give a verbal response, or in an incident which Michael needed the help of the teacher, he was sure to respond with a drawn-out, stuttering episode.

Mason learned to sense the student's aversion to situations of interacting with him; they led to a troubled response. He gave Michael the opportunity to speak at his own pace. Also, as a result of my recommendations, Mason asked the entire class to suspend play for a few moments.

When they quieted down, he told the class "I am interested in helping Michael overcome his stuttering. I want the cooperation of the whole class. In this way, my client made allies of the class in helping the stuttering student feel more at ease.

As aggressive as the group was, something was touched inside their hearts that brought the individuals together for this common goal. In addition, Michael felt cared for by his peers and his teacher.

Putting aside their habitual approach of taunting and provoking, they listened sympathetically as the youngster tried to express himself. The group was working as a unit in helping the student to improve his ability to communicate.

The group's willingness to share their time freed the boy to drop some of his negative defenses in his speech pattern. This allowed the group more access to the real person behind the stuttering; it was an individual that they cared about.

The students demonstrated their empathic ability, and the empathy was accepted by Michael who needed support.

My client was able to make the class work as a unit in a common cause and this gave the feeling of trust among the members.

During the fall semester, Michael could not express himself without constant stuttering. Mason understood the pupil's speech difficulty probably was related to his Life Story. Michael might have had strong and forceful parents who placed the child under great stress.

Mason tried to make his classroom atmosphere be relaxed and nurturing. As the term progressed, Michael's problem was ameliorated significantly by the less-intrusive way my client had chosen to establish contact with him.

By the spring semester, his speech cleared up, and he was able to enunciate rather clearly to explain what was bothering him. Mason understood that the emotional support from his peer group was what Michael needed to confront an authority figure.

The students from school represented a caring unit and this unit was compassionate and understanding. The class and Mason were displaying concern for Michael's problem, demonstrated by listening to him without placing any extra pressure or making fun of him.

The class and the teacher attempted to comprehend how the pupil was verbalizing his feelings and gave him support. Their mere quiet presence was reassuring. Mason's efforts assisted the group's relationship, and created productive surroundings in meeting the student's needs.

Even though my client had dysfunctional parents, he came to realize that his family relationship was not the norm. Seeing parents who were concerned with their children made him believe that he had the ability to be a loving husband and a good father.

Before his teaching experience, Mason believed that he did not have the ability to be a success because his parents always criticized him and never complimented him.

His first year of teaching opened his eyes; he recognized that he is a caring individual. By working with the students, Mason accepted and understood that his parents were incapable of love yet he was able to change that pattern of behavior.

Start on your quest to look behind your personal closed doors to find answers. The first step to escape your abyss is to admit you have hidden problems. Step two is recognizing that you have the ability to move away from your strife. You do not have to repeat the negative aspects in your Life Story. Your

life is yours. You get to decide everything; it is your
choice.

> Everything in life is a learning experience,
> and the information you learn from others
> can give you the power
> to move in the right direction.

Making Trouble For Yourself

Inner reflection is similar to cleaning out a closet; you don't always know what you will discover. If you cannot, or will not, use the items in your closet, donate them or get rid of them. In other words, clean out all the junk in your closet.

In a similar manner, your past experiences are *hanging around*. If these memories and experiences serve you, great—continue to keep them as valuable assets in your life. After all, they serve as an indicator to what may occur in your future.

On the other hand, if you are holding on to old, negative occurrences, accept and learn from what happened in order to move forward in a new way.

> *There is a small gap*
> *between childhood and adulthood,*
> *and your Life Story is setting the stage*
> *for today.*

JOHN'S LIFE STORY OF INABILITY TO EXPRESS EMOTIONS

John was a teacher in his mid-thirties and recently married. He came into therapy to overcome his fear of mirroring his dysfunctional parent's marriage. As a youngster, he overvalued his parents' ability to be kind and generous. It probably was his method to protect himself from anxiety associated with hurtful feelings towards his parents, who he feared.

During the early 1970's the New York City Board of Education started to lay off thousands of teachers.   Worry surrounded John about his job security.

During this stressful economic period of time, many teachers felt they had no security, and any position in a school seemed to be a blessing.   There appeared to be no protection from layoffs, and the Board of Education was going through difficult times.

Since my client was not a senior teacher, he lost his job; however, his principal obtained another teaching position for John at a junior high school in Harlem.

Since he was married, John was glad to have any job. In the back of his mind, he knew he could lose his position at any time.

John's new position was not in social studies, which he had been teaching. He was to teach English with an emphasis on reading.   His new principal informed him that his classes would consist of students who were held over once and some of them were held over twice for low reading scores.

He also said, "Oh yeah, just keep them from wrecking the school." He gave John the impression that educating them would be hard because of their history with behavior problems.

John related the following to me.   "When I entered the classroom, I introduced myself.   As I proceeded to write my name on the chalkboard, I was hit on the back of my head with a piece of chalk, and the class laughed in an uproar.

"I had difficulty restraining myself because during childhood, my mother constantly hit me for any misgivings. I learned not to tolerate any disobedience, and she taught me to confront it with a violent rage. Although I don't consider myself a violent person, I often automatically react with anger."

77

John went on to say that he heard my advice in his head, and in a split-second, he decided not to act on how he felt.

"I allowed myself to feel angry but I didn't react or behave on that emotion. Dr. Wallach, you taught me a very important concept for life. Go by what makes sense, not how you feel."

As I explain to my clients, sometimes what makes sense and how you feel are in agreement, but sometimes these emotions are not in agreement. When this happens, it is hard to control ourselves and we must learn to work on the latter.
Feeling the rage and not acting upon emotions is helpful in reaching a successful outcome. Take the power to overcome this emotion.

John's instincts warned him there could be potential trouble with this class. He decided to step back, watch and try to understand the pupils' reactions. Taking the pressure off of him, he decided not to talk and figure out his next move.

His silence represented a number of different communications for each class member. The silence was the beginning of an uncertain communication process that the students were not equipped to handle.

Most of them were worried about making a statement to John, inviting feedback they could not handle; therefore, it was the moment most students dread. Everyone remained silent for a while hoping my client would give them some sort of signal to his intentions.

Studying the students' reactions, John could make a plan of attack. Finally one student asked, "Why aren't you yelling at us?"

John replied, "Why should I do that?"

The student answered by saying that the job of a teacher is to get the class into trouble with the principle when they misbehave. My client responded by saying that he didn't want to get anyone in trouble today.

Again the class was silent because they didn't know what to do. The ringleaders of the class, mostly male, got together in the back of the room for a talk.

One student named Carl led the group. He was muscular, tall and an intelligent young man with leadership qualities. The class didn't know what to do because most teachers would have taken the bait and punished them. Not giving the class the usual response confused them.

John realized he had warded off their attack and they didn't know what to do or think about him.

The students were getting a little anxious which gave my client time to study the situation. Thinking about his next move would be directed on their next means of action.

John was starting to get on familiar grounds—similar to his childhood experiences of figuring his mother's next physical or emotional response.

The class continued with Carl leading the dialogue by stating, "You shouldn't be sitting down. You get paid for teaching, not sitting."

Another student exclaimed, "You will get into trouble if the principal comes in and sees this."

My client reminded them that they were all deficient in their reading levels and stood a good chance of being left back again. He mentioned the principal was aware of this fact.

John continued, "The principal knows that the class has poor behavior and poor test scores. You need me more than I need you."

The class threatened him, "If you don't teach, we will wreck the room."

My client replied, "I am willing to help you with your reading grades, but I will not teach if you destroy the room or misbehave."

The class had another private conversation, and then demonstrated what the principal was talking about; they threw chairs and turned desks over. Simultaneously, they carefully tore the material from the bulletin board.

When they "neatly" pulled down the material, John knew he was gaining ground. The pupils were testing their limits and testing his responses. John decided to take out his newspaper and read. This created even more havoc, but he held his position and waited for their next move.

The group had another discussion; they didn't know what to do. Carl yelled, "You should be teaching us."

My client told Carl that he should have said, "Please teach."

Amazingly, the entire class, in unison, repeated, "Please teach us."

John responded that before starting on the lesson, they would need to please put the room back the way it was.

They did it in record time. John explained to them that he would try to improve their reading scores but they must cooperate and act correctly.

This was an opportunity for Emotional Education. John attempted to express his empathic responses to their concerns as they were raised and took care not to express judgment on their actions. The teacher had built a position of devising a positive

relationship, and he was able to reach the students on their ability to behave correctly.

The class started to move into a healthier direction in which they viewed the teacher as the leader and the person in authority.

John verbally returned to the goal of helping the class to pass the New York City reading test. When he returned to this issue, he directly pointed out this goal was important; therefore, the class should be involved with the direction of improving their reading grades.

John realized this group of children did not know how to properly ventilate their internal anger. The only means they knew was by acting out in an inappropriate manner.

John used my directions in therapy. The first step in teaching is to change the negative behavior to a positive one. My client asked the students that if they felt like doing something destructive, he would like it if they would tell him and not act it out.

John gave an example, "If the class gets upset with something, someone or even me, they should verbally express these emotions in words not in actions. If someone feels like throwing a chair, it would help if he would say, 'Mr. Reynolds, I feel like throwing a chair because I can't get you to do what I want."

The class was learning Emotional Education. It was teaching the students to put their thoughts and feelings into words. John taught them that they can control their actions through verbalization. Using my advice, he mentioned their emotions did not control them, and they have the power to control their actions.

It is not unusual for class members to revert back to their older inappropriate behavior due to fear of moving to a successful outcome. This fear of success

81

can be eliminated when the group is at ease with everyone. Most people think it would be unwise to rush right into a new environment until they know how their thoughts are going to be treated: whether these ideas will be met with support or met with confrontation, whether or not it is alright to share their real emotions and concerns to others.

The students began to verbalize their thoughts and emotions to John. He empathized and thanked them for the communication. The pupils became comfortable in the new classroom setting.

This process can cut down on destructive behavior and replace it with productive behavior. Helping the class emotionally, my client was able to teach the appropriate lessons in reading.

My client stated that he wanted to improve their scores, but he felt uncomfortable because he hadn't figured out how he could assist them. During the semester, the class found out that John was not a teacher of English or an expert on reading skills.

One student said, "You probably didn't have to know how to read and that is why you became a social studies teacher." The class laughed hysterically expecting John to retaliate with a reprimanding remark.

Instead, he also laughed because it was funny. My client handled remarks similar to this with compliments for expressing how they thought.

Emotional education is defined by sharing feelings. The students must share their emotions with the teacher, and the teacher needs to try to understand and not criticize the students' expressions. Through these means, harmony can be accomplished between all parties. Thus, many behavior problems can be eliminated, and the teacher can move forward into the true education process of teaching.

The result of Emotional Education is that students feel more cared for. The old fashion theory of verbal criticism, used by the teacher, does not work and usually causes disharmony in the classroom.

Through our therapy sessions, John was better able to tolerate what the pupils were communicating in school, and he was gaining insight into understanding their perspective.

One student poignantly verbalized that Mr. Reynolds didn't know what it was like living in Harlem. The pupil said, "I feel like a prisoner, and my parents are the guards. I have two good parents; my father earns a good living as a mailman. After school, my parents don't want me to stay outside because the drug addicts are shooting up under the staircase of the building." He continued, "Everyone in this community is harmed by the few people who don't obey the rules."

John explained that the student's parents were concerned over his safety, and they were only trying to protect him from the evil influences in the neighborhood.

Hearing similar stories about their lives, John realized the students felt relaxed enough to tell him their day-to-day problems at home and in the community. Being heard by an adult made them feel at ease; they were able to concentrate more on studies than on their problems and stresses of everyday life.

When teacher-student relationships are positive, they strengthen the cooperation between both parties. If they are negative because of direct or indirect clues of hostility or lack of trust, barriers are erected between both parties and there is little progress.

In therapy, John told me he wanted to help these students. Most of the pupils were good children in a bad situation. He wasn't sure how he could assist them, but he knew he had to accept their circumstances. Also, he felt inadequate because this was the first time he was teaching reading.

I mentioned to him that he was picking up how the students felt about themselves, and my client agreed. The students and my client were feeling trapped by the situation.

Through my intervention, he decided to take this problem, break it down into smaller parts, and attack each part individually.

First, he asked his students how they felt about the reading test. They responded that they didn't feel they could pass because they felt stupid.

Second, he realized the books given to him were boring. He knew he would have to find interesting reading comprehension books to get their attention.

Third, he located an unused storeroom in the school where there were many books; he found exactly what he needed. A set of books for different reading levels entitled *Real Stories* would serve his purpose. These books consisted of interesting short stories with comprehension questions at the end of each unit. The books were for the fifth through the eighth grade levels.

Fourth, he used these books every day in class. The students read out loud and everyone was given a chance to read. The rules were set that no one would make fun of another student's reading ability. At the end of each chapter, the class tackled the questions.

The class worked together as a unit to understand the right answers to the questions. As pupils improved, they became more confident and reading levels increased.

The students were making progress in their behavior and in their academics, but an opportunity arose for John.

During the middle of the year, he was lured into another teaching job closer to his apartment in Brooklyn with the promise that it was a wonderful job. The education supervisor who wanted him for this position did it under false pretenses. At the time, John was unaware of his contribution to the situation.

JOHN'S THEME OF BETRAYAL AND PRACTICING NEW COMMUNICATION THROUGH EMOTIONAL EDUCATION

During a therapy session, he realized he was reliving one of his childhood betrayal themes. John thought the new supervisor was trustworthy but she was similar to his cunning and deceiving parents.

He was returning back to a situation which was familiar to him—being taken advantage of. The supervisor was not looking out for his or the students' best interests. She probably was motivated by her own personal agenda and used my client to accomplish her plan.

Falling into this woman's trap caused distress for everyone. Making trouble was easy for John because he learned this concept from his parents, who were experts on troublemaking.

Before John left his Harlem school, he told the class he was leaving to go to another school. At that time, the class never expressed any negative feelings

85

towards his departure. The class was in denial; they refused to discuss the ending of their alliance.

The students' denial was rooted in the fact they cared very much, but were not in touch with their emotions or their ability to verbalize these feelings. It was an abrupt closure for them, and this ending was perceived as a form of rejection on my client's part.

According to my client, the new job situation in Brooklyn was an unforeseen nightmare. The principal wasn't satisfied with the previous teacher assigned to the class, and the students didn't want to accept my client as their teacher. John was reliving his childhood again; the supervisor had placed him in a familiar, but uncomfortable, position which was similar to his childhood of not being wanted.

After the first three days, John knew it was not going to work to his benefit or to the benefit of the new students.

At my suggestion, he called his former principal and asked to return to Harlem. Luckily, the principal allowed him to come back.

Upon returning after three days, John heard from the faculty that his former class had wrecked the school. The first replacement teacher lasted five minutes because one of the students exposed himself to her; she ran out of the building and never returned. The class took the fire extinguishers off the walls and sprayed the hallways.

When John entered the room, the students stated that they missed him and reported, in a laughing manner, that they had been on excellent behavior during his absence. The class gave my client a tough time for the next few days.

He questioned, "I thought you were glad to see me." They agreed, and yet continued to say that they were not going to make it easy on him for abandoning them.

John felt that many of these students had hostile feelings which were related to their own Life Story. This school environment was similar to their home environment; they were probably abandoned by a parent and/or parents. They centered their anger upon him for doing the same thing.

John, with my advice, went back to the Emotional Education concept. In the case of anger and rejection, the teacher should reach past the indirect expressions and encourage students to verbalize any of these feelings directly to the responsible individual.

The teacher needs to acknowledge the validity of the emotions and should not attempt to talk the pupils into feeling differently.

John went around the room and asked each student how he personally felt about the departure and the return. The pupils expressed a wide range of emotions from hurt, belief that he did not care for them, and feeling abandoned.

This exercise helped them to say what they were expressing through actions.

When John apologized, they calmed down and they were ready to start back on their reading skills.

He saw through his students' eyes how not feeling cared for can lead to turmoil. As the semester progressed, the class continued with the routine of working with the reading comprehension books.

John realized his error in leaving had the effect that the students didn't feel safe in the school environment. My client became totally committed to them, and he worked hard for their progress.

In return, they were improving their skills and wanted to do well on the city-wide reading test. They became more confident, and were obtaining the skills to pass.

The process of understanding Emotional Education and how to use this concept in everyday life made my client feel he was on the path to success in his work and in personal relationships.

At the end of the school year, a senior teacher of English said to him, "You did it." He explained that 20 of John's 22 students graduated due to passing reading scores. His group had advanced more in reading from the previous year than any other English class in the building.

Later in John's teaching career, he learned that he had taught that class incorrectly. Instead of having students read out loud, the teacher is the one who should read out loud and the class follow along. Even with his error in teaching skills, the majority of the class passed the reading test.

It appeared that the combination of a good relationship between the teacher and students. through Emotional Education, the concept of feeling cared for, and practicing reading skills led to a positive outcome for the class. The majority of the class graduated and went to high school.

At the end of the school year, my client was still in the process of learning about the relationship between caring and success.

After that year's tumultuous, negative experiences, he became more relaxed with the impression that he was capable of being in caring relationships. He realized he could change his past behavior and had the ability to be a nurturing and loving individual.

Creating an Emotionally Stable
Life at Home

Many of my clients feel confused and angry when they cannot understand where their emotions are coming from. When they can state the problem, it can be more easily solved.

> *People want happiness but they don't know, in general, how to get it. Your future is unwritten so be your own author and write it the way you want it to be. Your possibilities are endless.*

Marriage is an institution that is filled with balancing acts of working hard to afford necessities and finding quality time to be together. A male client in his late thirties was in a similar situation with his family. His wife, Cynthia, worked part time and his two children were in daycare.

HENRY'S THEME OF DETERMINATION NOT TO REPEAT HIS PARENTS' DESTRUCTIVE MARRIAGE PATTERNS

The young couple bought a house, and both had to work hard to pay the mortgage. The husband worked two jobs and attended graduate school for his master's degree. He came home, exhausted, late at night.

Henry reported to me that his wife would come downstairs from the bedroom into the kitchen and update him about her day. Cynthia would tell him about her part-time job, the children, and basically unload on him because she felt overwhelmed.

Many husbands and wives go through this situation, and on some level, it can be viewed as a positive situation.

Henry's wife wasn't keeping thoughts to herself. Keeping unpleasant experiences cooped up in one's mind has the possibility of causing illness. Verbalizing thoughts is helpful to an individual's well-being.

On the other hand, Henry was feeling over-burdened by the intensity of his day and he wanted to share his thoughts. Feeling drained, he wanted to update her and verbalize his hard-working day.

When he tried to tell her how he felt, it led to arguments; Cynthia felt her life was strenuous and she couldn't handle his problems. She wasn't ready to hear him because she was juggling many chores, and it was difficult.

Their home environment didn't mirror the happy family sitcoms on television, and the friction between them made the children uncomfortable.

There was trouble ahead for all of them. Henry came from a family with poor control issues. When Henry's father came home from work, he fought with his mother if dinner wasn't on the table or if he didn't like the meal.

His father yelled at the children constantly. His father often said, "Children should be seen and not heard." Henry did not want to repeat this past with his wife and children.

Unfortunately, the turmoil was affecting his four-year-old son who started to act out his stress in nursery school. His son's school called because the child was acting strangely. This was Henry's wake up call.

91

According to his teacher, Henry's son had been a friendly, out-going boy who played well with others; but this day he was found sitting under a desk and not socializing with the other children. This situation had occurred after Henry had a huge argument with his wife. At the nursery school, his son was hiding from all the noise in the classroom.

Speaking to me about this situation, Henry realized that he had to correct the dysfunction in his family.

Verbal arguing causes anxiety which produces a powerful impact on the internal system of each family member, and his son was demonstrating this turmoil.

The family's role is to support its members, and this support can be hampered by problems in communication. A lack of communication can lead to stress and the result is that the family unit cannot carry out its function.

I stated that one should be persistent and not expect success to come quickly. Success often comes slowly and it is helpful to get the other person thinking about the situation to improve it.

I told my client he should distract himself from feeling sorry, accept the situation, and turn it into a positive one. Henry finally realized after creating friction with his wife, that he would have to take accountability to fix the situation.

> *If you really want to do something,*
> *you can find a way to succeed.*

Henry wanted to get out of distress and not get deeper into misfortune.

In the back of Henry's mind, he realized that cancer was rampant on his wife's side of the family, especially with the females. Cynthia's mother, her aunts and her female cousin had been diagnosed with various forms of cancer.

During this stressful period of time, his wife went in and out of the hospital to remove precancerous conditions in various parts of her anatomy.

Believing that stress could be a cause for cancer, Henry needed to emotionally nurture his wife until she felt cared for enough to even ask him about his day. This was hard for him, but knew it was better than having turmoil at home or having an ill wife.

For six months, Henry listened and consoled his wife. It was difficult because he arrived home around ten o'clock in the evening on weekdays; he also worked in the morning on weekends.

On weekend afternoons, he spent the rest of the day with his family without talking about his problems. Through this process, life greatly improved at home.

The most important concept Henry learned was to stop arguing with his wife regarding her parenting skills. Before accepting this concept, Henry often questioned his wife about her decisions.

Realizing he could act like his father by demanding and acting like a boss, he knew it was wrong to proceed in this manner. He had to act on what made sense and not how he felt.

Previously when my client questioned his wife's opinions on how to raise the children, she felt criticized. The children picked up this negative feelings and misbehaved.

After recognizing the troubled situation, the treatment was easy to implement an emotional equilibrium to the family.

I helped Henry understand that a role of the father is to support the mother with what she thinks is best for the children. A mother's instinct is generally a better gage than the father's feelings, assuming she spends more time with the children.

I helped Henry to see that, basically, the only time a father should intervene is if a mother is physically or emotionally harmful to a child or placing a child in a dangerous situation.

Learning more lessons in marriage through our sessions, my client discovered that many women need a break from the daily chores of rearing the child and doing housework. Women need a small vacation from their daily routine.

Henry determined that a husband needs to reach out by emotionally and physically supporting his wife. He needs to get involved with the entire family because one person cannot do it all.

Henry related that in his childhood his parents never helped each other; they acted more like strangers than a family unit. He now realizes this was the wrong way to behave.

Helping one's spouse is a good opportunity for the father to take the child out to a park or to help with household duties.

It is good for children to see cooperation between parents on activities because it will be to their benefit when they have to cooperate with others in school and in life. His support for his wife continued.

Finally she asked him, "How was your day today?" The ice was broken so Henry gave her some information.

When he came home from work, she continued to ask him about his day; eventually, my client was able to share with her freely. A happy wife and children leads to a happy marriage.

This established the stable environment that Henry wanted for his family and the turmoil was over. Everyone in society seeks to feel secure in life and gratify his desires.

Unfortunately, there are forces which interfere with this wish. When you realize these outside influences can be managed, your hopes will not diminish. If you are patient, tranquility can be the result.

Henry related that he can comfortably say he now has a very good marriage because they help each other. His wife is his best friend and they equally share their thoughts.

It took years of patience and work to establish this happy relationship. As a couple, they had to go through difficult situations to reach this point.

He acknowledged his Life Story was influencing his thought process. Realizing this fact, he cut a new path for himself by controlling his actions; he behaved according to what made sense for a happy outcome. In doing so, he had a positive response from his wife.

Another client had a breakdown in communication with his wife that caused him strife.

A male client, in his late thirties with a receding hairline, told me his wife was having severe menstrual pain during her monthly cycle. Eric explained, "Her doctors are not able to help her with any medication and they can't find anything physically wrong with her."

He asked me to talk to her for one session to see if I could figure out what was really going on in her head to make her so ill.

MARIE'S LIFE STORY OF NEEDING
TO BE ACKNOWLEDGED AND HEARD

When Eric's wife came into my office, I saw an attractive lady with sandy blond hair and blue-green eyes. Marie was a mother of two children under the age of seven, a boy and a girl. She explained that she was contemplating having another child.

"My husband doesn't want to have another baby," she blurted out, "and he refuses to discuss the matter with me."

I asked myself, *Could an emotional reaction to not being understood affect the menstrual cycle?*

I suggested to Eric that I thought the problem wasn't with his wife's health but perhaps with him. His inability to discuss having another child with his wife made her believe she wasn't cared for.

She unconsciously displayed her anger over this situation, and it manifested in her monthly cycle. Of course the manifestation of having a child and her monthly cycle is biologically related.

I recommended that Eric have a discussion with Marie on the idea of having another child.

He responded that he felt uncomfortable with the topic. Also, he related that his parents never discussed anything. "On weekdays, my Mom was in charge and on weekends my Dad was in charge of family plans." Eric could see how his past was influencing his present.

96

I further explained it was my impression that Marie really didn't want the third child; she just liked the idea of thinking what the child would be like.

He wasn't sure how to even have a discussion with her on this topic. I suggested that when she wanted to talk about it, he could just ask general questions. For instance, "Would you want a boy or a girl? Would the child be a scholar or an athlete? Would the child be tall or of average height? What names do you like?"

Eric followed my advice, and his wife talked about the topic more and more.

In another session, Marie mentioned, "I feel more understood and cared for by my husband, especially when we talk about another baby."

As they discussed the topic more, Marie's heavy bleeding and cramps were subsiding. About nine months later—enough time to expect and deliver a child—she mentioned to Eric that she was no longer having excessive bleeding or pain. I wondered if these discussions resolved the emotional resistance behind the symptoms.

She also thanked him for discussing the idea of another child and told him that she realized, at this stage of her life, she didn't want the responsibility of taking care of another child.

Marie never suffered from menstrual symptoms again.

The conflict was eliminated and their marriage greatly improved. Eric became comfortable talking to his wife; and in my opinion, a good marriage is when two people help each other and communicate their emotions.

> *You won't move forward unless you take time*
> *to understand where you have been*
> *and where you want to go.*

You have the power to get through any situation if you think about your desired outcome. Communication between partners is important, and it is beneficial that the communication be non-judgmental.

In a good relationship, the partners learn when to take the lead and when to step back and let their partner lead.

The marriage structure constantly changes and people take on different roles—sometimes it is about money, household duties, taking care of the children or taking care of the other person. In other words, it is about taking care of the emotional side of the relationship and being flexible.

Once you become aware of your inner power to avoid trouble, your newly-founded freedom will evolve to focus on your goals.

Sometimes People Give You Troublesome Feelings

If you are an observer of life, you can learn about yourself and others. Looking at people's behavior is like viewing a tool box full of information. These tools help you understand where an individual is coming from and perhaps the direction she or he is heading.

When another person's behavior is out of the norm, he might be acting out a situation which he is going through and cannot express verbally.

Therefore, the behavior—whether good or bad—is a reflection of his Life Story. When you can understand another's emotions, you can deal with them appropriately.

BEN'S LIFE STORY OF LEARNING SURVIVAL TECHNIQUES

A young male client in his early thirties with dark curly hair and an athletic build was faced with trouble in understanding other people's motives.

With his educational background, he obtained a high school teaching position in special education for emotionally handicapped students. Ben was placed in a situation where he had a lot of personal experience—that of being in a troublesome environment.

His Life Story was tumultuous because his father and mother were constantly battling. If they were not fighting with each other, they took out their aggression on my client.

The only relief Ben obtained was when he went to school or to sleep. His childhood was similar to a soldier walking through a minefield; he did not know when his parents would blow up, and there was no one to help when an explosion occurred. Ben's story consisted of survival; he was walking on eggshells until he was old enough and financially able to move out on his own.

Ben's principal in the Brooklyn high school didn't want the special education program in his building. My client believed the principal was afraid that special education pupils might contaminate the general education students. Ben was one of three teachers who worked with three special education classes; these pupils were classified as either learning disabled or emotionally handicapped.

In the 1970's this was a new situation on the high school level; these students joined with the general education population in hallways and in the cafeteria. Previously, these pupils had been placed in separate schools away from the general population.

Ben related the principal thought it would help to keep special education pupils separated from the general population as much as possible. The principal decided to keep the two classes on separate floors at different ends of the building because he hoped the students wouldn't socialize with each other.

The school had a large population and at lunch time there would be a thousand students in the cafeteria. Due to programming, all the special education classes had the same lunch period.

Ben noticed that a phenomenon occurred by the middle of the year. The special education students gravitated towards each other, and they ate lunch in the same section of the cafeteria and at the same tables.

The first day of school was a memorable one. My client entered the classroom and introduced himself. A large male student shouted from the back of the room, "I hate you and I am going to throw a chair at you."

After months of my teaching and training, Ben understood the principles of Emotional Education. He asked the student, "Would you like to throw a chair from the front of the room or from the back of the room?"

His emphasis was on the chair rather than on the student's desire, intent or feelings. In other words, my client took an object-oriented position with the student. To his relief, the young man finally sat down, defused, and commented, "You're crazy. No one ever said that to me before."

At the end of their first morning together, the pupil approached my client, apologized, and said, "I think maybe I can talk to you."

He said that his parents were in the process of getting a divorce, and his father had thrown him out of the house for a couple of hours the previous night. By relaxing him, Ben was able to lay the foundations for what turned out to be a long and productive relationship.

The amazing part of this story is the fact that this student was carrying over Ben's own childhood experiences. The emotion the student induced in Ben reminded him of what happened with his father.

Ben had felt like putting the student out of his room and that was exactly what his father did. Ben was glad he didn't take what the student said personally, and he was able to work with this situation as it presented itself.

At lunchtime, my client learned from other teachers that this angry, physical sixteen-year old had managed to get dismissed from most of his other classes.

Of course this occurrence not only happens in the classroom; it can happen anywhere in life.

People experience their past all the time in various situations. They see you as someone in their past or present life, and they react to you in a similar manner as if you were this other person.

> *The emotional relationship which develops*
> *between people is sometimes based on attitudes*
> *left over from a previous experience*
> *or from a current situation.*

As the individual on the receiving end of these unexpected emotions, you can be quite confused. Many times it isn't easy to distinguish between what you are feeling and why another person is acting out his Life Story with you. This concept takes a while to figure out, but in the long run it is beneficial.

Ben received an advanced degree in education, and was recommended for a promotion within the special education department in New York City. Not only did he not get the job but he almost lost his current teaching position.

One day in the high school hallway, Ben glanced at the newly-assigned supervisor in charge of his promotion. The supervisor appeared to act like Ben's parents, who wanted him out of their sight. It didn't make sense, and caused Ben many problems in keeping his job.

Just the mere sight of Ben seemed to arouse negative emotions in the supervisor that were transferred onto Ben.

Ben was transferred to a school which the supervisor wasn't in charge of—now he was out of the supervisor's sight. However, the entire experience made my client begin to relive his Life Story. Similar thoughts and feelings he had as a child appeared without warning. It made Ben feel anxious and uncertain about his future.

These thoughts or feelings can induce either positive or negative reactions within an individual. In my client's case, it was a negative reaction...a part of his past that he didn't want to relive.

Ben unintentionally had gotten involved with a person similar to his parents. He was frozen with fear as if he were a child again. He did not know how to handle the situation and just went along with it. Ben had been physically abused to the point where he almost died by his mother's hands.

A year later, the power structure in the New York City Board of Education changed, and Ben managed to secure a transfer to a school closer to his home.

In the new school, he met another tall male colleague, and mentioned this story to him. The colleague laughed, saying, "I understand because the same supervisor tried to make trouble for me."

Since his colleague didn't have malicious parents, he was able to handle the supervisor. He wasn't afraid of the supervisor, and the colleague was able to deal with the situation as it presented itself.

He told Ben that he pulled the supervisor to the side and explained that he wanted to keep his position. "I don't want you to bother me about my performance. I will make out a grievance with the union if you continue to annoy me, and I will expose you as the wicked person you are." The supervisor left him alone.

The colleague continued to say he discovered why the supervisor was negative to tall, well-built men. When the supervisor was thirteen-years old, his good looking, tall father deserted the family and left them in poverty. The family felt destitute. Since then, the supervisor hated and tried to destroy tall, handsome men.

Ben's physical image triggered this supervisor into action with hostile feelings. The representation gave the supervisor's past a visual reproduction and negative energy was discharged. His mental image guided his behavior.

Since he couldn't deal directly with his father, he indirectly was dealing with his anger through other men.

The story of a person's life and how much he did or did not feel cared for relates to the amount of misfortune he will experience for himself and the amount of distress he might cause others. It was an act of retaliation on behalf of the supervisor towards tall men.

During this nightmare my client was able to relive the worst moments of his childhood, but he did not act out his hostile emotions; he verbalized these feelings to me.

Ben was able to come through this outrageous experience intact and faced his demons from his childhood. He realized that he had the power to conquer his fear.

Realize that you cannot completely control your outside environment. Understanding this concept can help you focus on goals that you want to accomplish. This will reduce your stress level. Once you become aware of your limitations, you can make wise decisions.

Being Right Is Not the Solution

The old adage, "Life isn't always fair," is quite true. Individuals through their experiences understand life follows this maxim. Not pursuing the idea of *what is right* can help you move on with your life, and it can enable you to adjust to different situations.

Throughout life you are experimenting with relationships. After each trial, you hope you will get favorable outcomes from your endeavors.

People have two ways of making a decision. One way is by thinking. We consider the possibilities on all sides, weigh them and decide which path to follow.

The second way is following feelings without concentrating on all the various aspects of a situation. Many people act upon their feelings and it can cause trouble.

Man has the power to control himself in different circumstances. He or she has the ability to make observations and judgments about other people's motives. Unfortunately, some people's motives can cause harm. It is important to understand distinctions among numerous motives.

ZACK'S THEME OF BEING ACCUSED WHEN HE IS INNOCENT

Zack was one of my clients, a man with a short stature in his early forties, who was an intermediate high school gym teacher in Queens, New York. Zack was the youngest in a large family. His siblings always blamed him for any misgivings in the family.

For example, if they were playing in the living room and a lamp fell, they claimed that it was Zack's

106

fault and he was punished. If someone ate all the fruit, he was condemned again.

Zack never spoke up to his parents; he wanted to keep harmony in the family. Being the *fall guy*, he also took this role outside the family structure. Zack was uncomfortable in this situation and came into therapy to change his life.

He understood that he kept repeating his past because it was familiar but it was causing trouble for him. He realized he had to watch out for other's intentions to keep out of trouble.

Zack encountered difficulty with an associate at work, and this associate could have unintentionally caused my client his job.

According to Zack, a male associate, Peter, in his late thirties had a sense of humor and a great personality. Both teachers instantly became good friends and on occasion they went out to dinner with their wives.

Early in the fall semester, during the first period of the school day, Zack was in charge of a small physical education class in a weight room which was located in the basement of the school. This room was isolated from most of the school's population. When the students were taking off their garments to prepare for class, my client had a visitor.

Peter, who was on a break, came into the weight room, with a cup of coffee, to visit. Peter stood at the other end of a long table where Zack was standing and taking attendance.

The students were ready to participate in a gym activity when the principal looked into the room and then departed.

107

Zack told his colleague he was in trouble, but Peter disagreed.

Later that day, my client found a note on his time card to see the principal before he left for the day. The principal was an older gentleman who was in his early sixties. He looked upon his staff as his family, and he was the father figure; therefore, a figure who did not want to be questioned about his motivation. The principal wore suits with a shirt and tie because he wanted to look professional and in charge.

When Zack walked into his office, the principal asked him to sit down. He stated, "I am very disappointed in you." The principal went on to say that he saw my client drinking coffee while he was teaching a lesson and this behavior was unacceptable. The principal had not noticed that my client had a visitor.

Zack realized that he hadn't had the coffee, but his colleague had.

In a split second, Zack had to decide what his goal was. *Should I tell him the truth and run the risk of suggesting he was wrong and perhaps infer he had imagined something or would I be in more trouble if I told him the truth?* Zack was in a serious situation, and he had to get out of it.

People in authority have power over us, and in a difficult situation it is challenging for a subordinate to truly reveal his reactions.

The authority theme of the principal which confronted my client could be classified as a struggle between the truth or following the principal's perception of the situation. Zack had to resolve the conflict between his relationship with a nurturing and demanding individual who was an authoritative symbol, similar to his parents.

In my client's observation, the principal had a reputation of being punitive if someone did not agree with him. Zack decided this was not the time to stand up for the truth because this was not a case of right or wrong. He felt it was a case of demonstrating to him who was in power.

Sometimes situations are just the way they are, and you have to deal with it the way it is presented. My client decided to accept whatever punishment the principal was going to hand out. He did not act on how he felt by explaining the truth.

Deciding the best way to stay out of distress was to apologize for drinking coffee, Zack stated he would never do it again during class time. The principal was satisfied that his teacher had learned his lesson and told him to leave.

I encouraged Zack to call his colleague that evening and tell Peter the whole story. Zack asked him not to come in to socialize in any of his classes.

Peter said, "When I visit, I won't bring coffee."

So Zack emphasized, "The principal was upset that one of his teachers was drinking coffee during class time. What would he think if there were a visitor during a lesson?"

Due to Zack's forcefulness, Peter understood the direction the principal was inclined to think and decided not to visit.

As Zack suspected, the principal looked into the room the next morning and smiled with approval. My client was out of trouble. Zack had achieved his goal without criticizing the principal's judgment.

In one of our sessions, Zack remembered the injustice he had as a child. After punishment his parents often said, "I hope you learned your lesson." He never spoke to his parents that his older siblings accused him unjustly. He never said a word to his siblings about being unfair. He just accepted the punishment to keep harmony.

Zack's decision in this situation, however, was not passive acceptance to create harmony. In this instance, standing up for himself by stating that the principal was mistaken would have been unwise and unproductive. He tried to refrain from having a confrontation. Zack just listened to the principal and did not talk.

> *A person has the power to influence circumstances; it depends a great deal upon his thought process and his goals.*

However, my client was able to tell his friend what he expected Peter's behavior should be in regard to his job security.

Through this process of thinking about his goal, Zack was able to make the situation better. He had choices, and he had the free will to choose his direction. It seems that he made the right choice.

After this experience with the principal and his associate, Zack was more confident in expressing his thoughts clearly to another individual. By speaking in a factual way to his friend, he did not harm their relationship.

Zack took control over his Life Story by conveying his wishes, and he did not have to dwell in self-pity as he did as a youngster. He took charge of his life.

110

You have the same power by analyzing a difficult situation, deciding upon your goal, and implementing your actions to lead to a successful outcome.

People Facing Trouble

Everyone has early memories which could be detrimental to one's well-being. Emotional Education attempts to change feelings and actions through talking because words are the best way a person has of expressing his emotions to himself and to others.

Each of us has tensions stored up throughout our life—some of these feelings are expressed openly and some are not. Holding emotions in can be dangerous. It is helpful to have your energies reorganized, understood, and released through verbalization.

Most people face dilemmas because of their life Themes. I was seeing a young married couple who had individual sessions with me.

CAUGHT IN ANOTHER'S LIFE STORY

The professional thirty-year old female client, Suzanne, explained how difficult it was to get her husband to complete a task for her. Victor would leave out an important detail or forget to complete it. She felt that, basically, he did not do it intentionally.

She was puzzled also about her mother-in-law's behavior. For example, her mother-in-law purchased some gym equipment for the couple's new home. When the mother-in-law discovered there would be a delivery charge, she didn't want to pay the extra money. In addition, the mother-in-law suggested the couple rent a truck to pick up the equipment.

I mentioned to Suzanne, "Now you know where your husband learned this behavior of never finishing anything he starts. I believe he grew up with this topic of incompletion in his family. Victor is just repeating

112

his Life Story with you. Maybe his mother was unintentionally repeating a topic from her childhood memories. If so, it was unconscious behavior on her part."

I explained that the origin of this troublesome matter wasn't so important. I felt she shouldn't take this situation personally. "When it occurs again, it wouldn't be to anyone's benefit to act in an angry manner."

I explained that her husband would continue this pattern of behavior until he is helped to re-write this part of his Life Story.

She asked, "How can I help my husband?" I suggested that she not criticize him for behaving this way; but when he does, it might be helpful to say, "When your mother bought the equipment, she was doing the best she could and I'm sorry you have to follow her example in not completing the task."

It was my opinion that she would have to repeat the above statement many, many times until her husband understands and actually hears what she is saying. Then his actions would change.

Suzanne thought it might be worth trying until he made the emotional connection and emerged from it.

In another session, the husband who is a professional man in his thirties asked, "Why am I so upset with my mother about not paying for the delivery charge?" His inclination was that it had nothing to do with the money.

I agreed with him; it wasn't the money. It is the idea of not finishing a task. I responded, "Not completing chores your wife asks you to do is the same

thing—you are upset with your mother's actions."
Victor began to empathize with his wife's frustrations.

I have observed behavior patterns which upset
an individual are similar to the pattern he displays
towards others. Unfortunately, the individual doesn't
see he is acting out similar methods of disappointing
and upsetting others.

Victor was interested in ways to handle his
mother in regard to the delivery fees or completing an
assignment.

I explained, "If one is upset with another person,
it doesn't mean it's a good idea to start discontent over
it."

I suggested that Victor pay the equipment
delivery charge and drop the matter, explaining, "Your
mother is re-enacting a familiar pattern of behavior
from her Life Story. In other words, don't stand on the
principle as to what you think is the correct response."
The main point is his mother bought the equipment as a
present.

Many behavior patterns are not a question of
right or wrong; it is just the way it is. I said, "If you
want to be upset about it, it isn't to your advantage to
feel it for too long. Understand it, emerge from it, and
let it go."

> *Letting go of anger and disappointment*
> *can reduce stress and boost your outlook on life.*

Sometimes people have difficulty accepting the
feelings they encounter from others whether these

114

emotions are negative or positive. Many people have trouble in feeling cared for because it is not familiar; they tend to push it away. I will never forget one woman I worked with who was a lovely woman in her late forties.

She was not clear where her life was headed because her husband died a few years ago and there were no children from their union. She felt isolated in her plight.

NANCY'S LIFE STORY OF FOLLOWING SOCIETY'S NORMS AND THEME OF INABILITY TO ACCEPT LOVE

She stated that she enjoyed walking and sitting in the park. One day when she was walking, she met a young man in his twenties. She exclaimed, "This man is young enough to be my son."

After a few harmless meetings in the park, they eventually became romantically involved. Nancy told me how people stared at them as they walked hand in hand.

In many matters people have mental images of what mankind expects from them. She believed that society would not be able to comprehend her new relationship. This gentleman did not fit the pattern others had in mind for a woman of her age; his image did not correspond with the general population's reality.

My client grew up in a climate that such a relationship was taboo, and her past was trying to dictate how she should proceed with her boyfriend.

It appeared this young man, Ted, was smitten with her and he introduced her to his parents who were upset with the age difference.

115

Ted's parents thought it was a crazy relationship and decided that they would cut him out of their will and disown him.

Nancy felt horrible for Ted's situation, and she did not want to destroy his relationship with his family. She tried to break up with him.

In another session, Nancy came into my office explaining that Ted said that he loved her and wanted to get married.

She expressed that she also had great love and affection for him. This session took place in the 1970's when such a relationship was not fully accepted by society. She talked at length about how wrong and silly this romance was. She could not tolerate others' views on the subject of a relationship and marriage to a younger man.

On some level as a widow, she thought that she didn't deserve to be happy again, and had to break off the courtship.

Breaking off the relationship with Ted started more unrest.

She reported that her ex-boyfriend became ill and went into the hospital. He asked her to visit him and she did. He stated, "If you don't marry me, I will probably die."

After doing examinations and tests, the doctors discovered all results were negative, and they were baffled that his vital signs were deteriorating quickly. The doctors found nothing physically wrong with him but his health was declining.

She asked what I thought. I replied, "He is dying from a broken heart."

There are thousands of people all over the world who suffer from aliments such as headaches, stomach aches, pains in the chest, dizziness, and the doctors never find out what is causing their illnesses.

I believed the young man's unsolved illness might be caused by his emotions related to both his girlfriend abandoning him and how his parents were treating him.

I could relate to the boyfriend's situation as a result of my childhood experiences of unloving parents. When I was a child, my mother had no compassion even though I told her I was afraid to be left alone for hours in the apartment. She walked out without a word of encouragement.

This situation made me believe I was unwanted. Therefore, I understood Ted's emotions, and how his health could be affected by the situation.

My client asked what she should do. I questioned, "Do you care enough about him to save his life?"

She responded that she did.

I continued, "If you have to marry him to save his life, would you do it?"

Nancy promptly responded that she would.

I told her she should marry him because I believed if she didn't that he would probably die.

Nancy told Ted that she would marry him. The doctors were amazed with his recovery, and Ted was discharged two days later. Their wedding plans were forthcoming and she thanked me, saying that she would be in for her next appointment.

Nancy never showed up or returned my phone calls. Her close friend told me she disappeared with Ted.

I believe she finally was able to accept the positive feelings her future husband gave to her but she wasn't able to verbalize them to her friends and family.

This couple could not accept and adhere to other people's reality; therefore, they moved to a place where they were not affected by their family and friends judgment that their union was a mistake.

They wrote a new chapter in their lives by moving away and starting over.

Sometimes people experience misfortune in their lives and just cannot express how they feel. They block memories out and unconsciously re-enact the Story of their Life.

PHYLLIS' LIFE STORY OF ABANDONMENT

Another client who is a young attractive female grew up in an environment where her parents were not getting along. Phyllis related the following experience which occurred when she was a child.

One night her father woke her up in the middle of the night and told her he loved her.

The next morning she discovered he left the family without any forwarding information. The family was taken by surprise.

As a young girl, Phyllis was convinced the reason her father left was because she wasn't pretty enough. She said, "My father would have stayed if I was pretty."

Unfortunately, this emotion of not being attractive remained with her throughout her adult life—she believed she did not deserve affection from any male. Of course, this couldn't have been farther from the true reason why her father left the family, but she couldn't see it.

118

It is an interesting phenomena, but not un-common, that it is difficult for a child to separate or distinguish the outside world from herself.

The child criticizes herself rather than the person responsible for the negative situation. This is especially true if it is a parent.

In the case of my client, she felt no anger towards the father for not acting in a responsible manner because she truly thought his departure was her fault. I told her this wasn't the case, and it had nothing to do with her looks, but she didn't believe me.

As an adult, Phyllis managed to locate her father and tried to establish a relationship. It appeared he was happy with the reunion and he introduced her to his new family. He promised to be fatherly and helpful towards her.

She started to feel cared for and while she was rebuilding this relationship, she told me that she believed she was attractive. When the father faltered on all the promises of help, she started to feel unattractive again.

One day when she came into the office for her appointment, Phyllis thanked me for helping her and stated that she would be leaving therapy.

I asked, "Do you need to surprise me with this sudden announcement of your departure the same way your father surprised you?"

She commented, "I never thought about why I am leaving therapy, but I feel compelled to do it."

I pointed out that the age her father left the family corresponded to the same amount of time she spent in therapy with me.

Sometimes people feel compelled to do things that repeat a chapter from their life. Most people are not aware of this compelling force.

Even though they might be aware of it on some level of consciousness, I do not believe it will necessarily stop them from acting out the behavior because they are in denial the event ever happened. People usually go by how they feel rather than what makes sense.

Phyllis agreed with my understanding of the situation. She also agreed she needed me to understand what she was feeling the night when her father left. She wouldn't give me the opportunity to help her through this experience.

I stated, "You certainly can stop your appointments, but I don't think you are emerging from your childhood experiences." She was just re-living this terrible situation with me.

I continued, "If you don't emerge from your past, you might have difficulty getting involved in a close relationship with a man."

She agreed but left anyway. Two years later, I saw Phyllis walking on the street and she looked thrilled to see me. We briefly talked and I asked how her love life was.

She turned red and said that she had a man in her life who wanted to marry her. She admitted, however, that she was too afraid to get close to him with the thought he might leave.

I told her that I was sorry she was so scared and if she wanted me to help her overcome this feeling, I would be glad to do so.

She never contacted me. I believe she needed me to empathize with her problem. It would have been far better for her to emotionally talk about the hurt her father instilled in her rather than having me feel it for her.

In any event, her distorted view of her father was hampering her ability to move on with her life. I hope Phyllis was able on her own to seek out a successful, close relationship with a man.

In the above stories, there is a common denominator which is a distortion of reality. As children we are raised by parents who have set opinions. If we alter from those opinions, it can give the feeling of being unsuccessful.

As adults we need to understand what we learned from our parents. Keep the positive points and disregard the negative, even though you may feel a bit guilty doing it.

> *People in general think that when they feel guilty*
> *they must be doing something wrong.*
> *This certainly is not always the case.*

Another reason for self-sabotage is that people do not remember much of what happened to them in their early years. Children do not have a large vocabulary to express their feelings; they use images which can be distorted.

The unconscious is a region in the mind that has stored-up feelings which are trying to get out. Many of these energies are attached to childhood images that are not words.

When a nonverbal emotion is stored or repressed, especially a sad one, it either detaches itself from the representation or attaches itself to another image already in the unconscious. This can often cause distress later in life.

If you don't practice Emotional Education on yourself and understand the Themes in the Story of your Life, you will continue to repeat them...until you no longer are content with the familiarity. First work on changing your actions, then the comfort and freedom will follow.

A Story of Uncaring Emotions that Caused an Eating Disorder

A person, just as a therapist, needs to understand the Story of a person's Life for a loving relationship. Ask respectful questions and listen carefully to the responses and emotional reactions.

For your own "self-therapy," recognize that whatever type of trouble comes your way, you can face it when you can understand it. You must dig down into your inner feelings. You need to reveal these emotions *to yourself* to comprehend them.

> *You may feel there is no way to rid yourself from a particular circumstance, but there is a way to escape. It can only occur when you realize how you arrived at this point in time.*

The past is the past and you cannot change it. You must take responsibility and work on the present to grow as an individual.

JANE'S LIFE STORY OF INABILITY TO EXPRESS NEGATIVE EMOTIONS AND A THEME OF PROTECTING HER MOTHER

A client, who I'll call Jane, wasn't allowed to express negative feelings in her family. Therefore, she repressed all angry emotions which manifested into serious health-related problems.

Jane is a slim, well-educated woman who became self-attacking. She felt hopeless, and developed an eating disorder. When I met her, she was in her

123

late twenties and had never been in a meaningful relationship with a man. I was her third analyst.

In my observation, Jane appeared thin for her medium height, was extremely anxious as evidenced by her constant leg movements, spoke haltingly and repeated her sentences over and over with a monotone quality.

It appeared she both desired and dreaded contact with me.

The theme of the first session was self-attack and low self-esteem. She revealed she neither liked the way she looked or felt. She simply did not like herself.

That matter-of-fact confession recreated the negativity of her upbringing and her present relationship with her parents. "Nobody wanted me, and I certainly could not blame them," she argued.

In response to my request for some historical background, she indicated that when she was four, her thirteen-year old sister died of a mysterious and unexplainable death two days after being admitted to a hospital. At that point Jane became an only child.

Her mother retreated into a world of her own, neither openly mourning the death of the elder child yet not being able to give up her memory.

Jane had no serious illness as a child and this redoubled her sense of guilt that she was the surviving child.

Jane embarked on a special journey from that point in time to be perfect in all ways. She felt a need to save her mother from any more unhappiness.

She became a model student, made honor classes, and skipped two grades in school. She dreaded the possibility of doing anything that might cause her mother to become sick and dedicated her life to keep her mother from becoming depressed.

124

In spite of her efforts, the mother increased her critical appraisals of Jane's dress, demeanor, work as a student, and her companions.

This criticism created the ability to keep Jane away and the mother could quietly wallow in her own depression. This demonstrated to Jane that one should not get in contact with feelings or share them with anyone else.

Over the years, Jane developed the feeling that her relationship with her parents was strangling her. The parents were not getting along well with each other.

If her father tried to approach his daughter in an affectionate way, the mother argued with him until he avoided the child. This communication to the daughter continued to emphasize that she was a burden and not wanted.

When she was ten, Jane's parents informed her that she was going upstate to a rural area to attend summer camp. Her parents ignored her pleadings not to go; they believed it would be in her best interests to have a summer away from home.

Jane did comply, but retched for three days straight while at camp. The staff was so alarmed that they sent her back home.

It was at the age of ten that Jane learned *throwing up* was one thing she had control over which her parents did not, and she got her wish to stay at home.

Our early therapeutic relationship was marked by positive, warm feelings. I had apparently repeated something from Jane's upbringing that was good for her.

I put her in a position where she had to control her relationship-destructive propensities. I did this by giving her structure with regular weekly appointments.

As the treatment progressed, she repeated questions like a broken record, and I explored them with a positive and warm empathy towards her.

After some time with each repeated request for advice, her resistance to grow became stronger and stronger, and I felt more and more tortured by her conversations.

I realized that my giving her any advice seemed to recreate the negative transactions with her parents which had fixated her growth.

She asked, session after session, whether she ought to get her hairstyle changed. I tried to change the discussion by asking her questions on other topics but she returned to the dilemma of hairstyles again and again. Beauty parlors and dresses were the subjects of discussion, with the intent to persuade me to give in and tell her what to do. Her complaints took on a gnawing quality.

The torture was an attempt on her part to get me angry so I would not care for her. She wanted me to show her I did understand her, and on the other hand, she wanted me to act in a similar uncaring fashion as her parents behaved.

I admit that I felt that way but did not act on those feelings.

The first years of her therapy were difficult. Jane was anxious much of the time, torturing herself with self-doubts and self-attacks while she tortured me.

It appeared she was not interested in improving. She wanted me to do something to accomplish this task, and in her mind, the requests for advice captured the possessiveness of her mission.

Jane felt if I could only answer her in a way that would make her feel better, everything would be all right. She was just as miserable when she got advice, and giving it seemed to be a repetition of her former home environment.

She continued to create and repeat the story of her negative environment through actions and behavior, as well as thoughts and feelings.

She re-enacted the same environment outside therapy. When her friends and colleagues said, "You look beautiful" or "That was a good answer," she would quickly reply, "You are just trying to be nice to me. You don't really mean that."

Jane could not accept a compliment. Her mother put the emphasis not on her daughter's sense of well-being and self-pride, but on externals. The focus was on objects or things.

Jane learned from her mother that her dress and how she looked were more important than she was. So when fellow adults commented on how pleasing she looked, she responded, "It's not me; it's the dress."

Near the end of the first year I took the opportunity to discuss the theme of caring whenever possible with her. We discussed the following topics. "Did you feel cared for? Should I care about you? What if I did care about you? What if I did not care about you?" My feeling at this time was that I was being tormented, but I also had an enduring empathy for her, the victim of crushing self-attacks. Jane had made it clear that any effort by anyone to show her concern would be considered toxic.

127

I showed Jane my concerned sentiment by patiently listening, exploring, and showing her I was willing to be investigated as an object. Her attitude towards me began a slow change to a more positive position.

She later recounted that she was able to stop repeating requests for advice because she was getting the experience; I was concerned about her and would not get rid of her.

After a year and a half, her torture towards me stopped. The context of our interactions altered markedly. She still asked for advice, but in a less arduous manner.

Her father died the second year Jane was in treatment with me. She called to let me know why she would not be attending the session. I offered my condolences and told her I would see her in two weeks.

Upon her return, Jane scolded me for not paying a call to the family during the mourning period; this was a new feature in our relationship. Jane was not accustomed to directing anger towards me, but circumstances forced her, and possibly permitted her to express her criticisms of me. She believed I did not sympathize with her loss.

Although her experience was an uncomfortable one, this was the first time she actively expressed her annoyance to someone and felt it was right to do so.

The environment created in the therapy apparently made her feel safe enough to emerge verbally in this fashion.

Later, she told me she realized it was all right for her to take the risk of verbalizing negative emotions towards me because she knew I would not criticize her for it. It did not mean she was a bad, unlovable child for speaking up.

When she was able to state that she was annoyed with me over her father's death, it was as if she was becoming aware that there was another person in the room with her. This was in contrast to the first year of treatment, when she was not sure if I cared about her or even if I was in the room with her.

In one session, Jane asked, "Why can't I grow up?" She added, "I always had to be perfect for my mother. She never recognized me."

During this time, Jane was binging on sweets and then throwing up in a highly organized and ritualistic manner. She would eat cakes, cookies, and candies, throw up in the toilet and clean up any signs of her activity. She was anxious until she forced the regurgitation of all she had eaten. Afterwards, she felt depressed and full of self-hate.

I asked, "What is behind the binging? What are the memories and feelings attached to those associations?" I felt Jane was using the bulimia to defeat me. The eating disorder was a way to effect a denial of the angry feelings and aggression.

The patient was not aware of how she was recreating a negative environment and acting in an incorrect manner. I had to teach her to act in a successful way by creating a positive environment based on how she spoke and interacted. Previously she had not been able to separate how she felt and how she acted.

The death of her father and her hostile feelings towards me was the beginning of her first lesson in which she could feel negativity and talk about it without vomiting.

129

Jane related a story to me. When she was thirteen-years old, she had vomited into the toilet bowl just before the family went to an affair.

Furious, the father said to her, "I cannot believe a daughter of mine would do such a thing." The vomit had more importance to him than the reason behind Jane's action.

After many sessions, Jane was able to comment on the affection that was developing between us. With great effort, she told me she would feel anxious if she could not see me. She stated, "I am so lonely. I am starting to feel I need people."

One association to this was a memory from her early years. Her mother was not feeling well after the death of the first child, and she was hospitalized. Jane was sent to her aunt's home for the summer.

According to her parents, this was considered a treat, since the aunt's house was magnificent. Jane found herself alone once she arrived there.

Her aunt had no children, and there were few families in the area. Missing her family and playmates, Jane repeatedly asked her aunt if she could go home.

The aunt replied, "How ungrateful; you should be ashamed of yourself." She was not able to feel any anger at that time towards her aunt because she felt the aunt's remarks were correct.

I understood this as a communication referring to her present-day dilemma. Jane could not feel her true emotions; she kept angry feelings inside. These sentiments were directed towards her inner self; the bulimia was a by-product of her anger. The ritual of her eating disorder was keeping her from verbalizing the feelings necessary to help her progress.

130

At this point, when Jane asked me how she looked, I fed her *emotional food* to see whether she could retain it. Therefore, this began the struggle to break the binging cycle.

I responded, "It does not matter how you look." Jane considered this assertion and told me that looks were all that mattered in the dating scene or in the social structure at work.

I expanded, "It does not matter how you look, if you let people see the real you."

Jane was starting to feel good about herself and her crushing self-attacks were lessening. She was getting stronger.

In one of her sessions, Jane asked me to solve a long-standing puzzle. She wanted to know why her best friend became more distant as Jane became more successful.

I asked whether she had ever brought this topic up with the friend.

Jane replied, "I would never do it. The anxiety about confronting her or someone similar to my mother would kill me. I'd die. I avoid feeling anxious."

Yet, her relationship with her friend bore the mark of control in the other direction: She explained that when her girlfriend wanted to go out, she controlled her by saying no.

"I was anorexic prior to bulimia. My parents pushed me to eat, and I ate. Then I started vomiting. That was the only thing my parents could not stop me from doing."

With her friend, the anxiety was so uncomfortable she was not able to assert herself, so she resorted to passive-aggressive behavior to recapture the element of power.

We returned to an idea I had shared with her previously. If she wanted to reach her goals, the thing to do was act correctly, even if she believed it was wrong. In this way, she could create the positive environment that would give her what she needed.

She was ready to apply this to her problems with her friend. Jane realized if she took a stand with her girlfriend, she would be more anxious but would get what she wanted.

The next sessions were used to investigate particular situations, and I gave her supervision on how to handle the girlfriend so a more complementary relationship could evolve.

In the process, Jane told me she was jealous of her friend because the friend reminded her of her sister, and she was repeating a negative experience from her early life.

"You are right," I responded. "Your sister died, she haunts you, and now your friend haunts you. She haunts you to get what she wants."

As balance entered that friendship, Jane reported greater satisfaction. In spite of the continued emphasis on memories, the intent was not to get information that Jane would share; the issue was more a dynamic one.

It is not necessarily coming up with memories that cure an individual. It is overcoming the resistance in producing memories that helps the individual move forward.

I started to think about how I could help repair what happened to her after the loss of her sister and the impact it must have had on her parents. I determined that somehow I would have to set up a

132

situation to help her verbalize her feelings towards me which she never felt or was able to verbalize towards her parents. Jane had to feel and verbalize her resentment to heal herself.

After a while in therapy, the opportunity to help her presented itself. It was time to play a game of chess with Jane.

I have a twenty-four hour, missed appointment policy with my clients. They are responsible for the session financially if they do not cancel their appointment within a twenty-four hour basis; the only exceptions are illness or a family death.

Jane called a few hours before her time to cancel. She said, "It's my birthday; I forgot to tell you. I know you will understand that I should not be charged. It would be like a birthday present."

The next time I saw her, she told me she enjoyed her birthday and she appeared sure I wouldn't charge her for the missed session. She had made her move so it was time for me to make mine.

I asked when she was planning to pay me for the missed session. She was shocked, "What?"

She was getting annoyed with me and demonstrated angry emotions. Her body was clearly agitated and her legs started to shake. She had never verbalized any annoyance directly to a person, especially a parental figure in authority.

Jane exclaimed, "What is the matter; shouldn't I celebrate my birthday?"

I responded, "Sure, but why should I have to pay for it?"

She retorted by asking me if I cared for her.

I replied by saying, "Are you trying to get out of paying my fee?"

133

She raised her voice to me for the first time and stated she couldn't believe I was doing this to her.

I spoke back to her by saying, "I cannot believe you don't appreciate me. I have to make a living by charging fees to my clients."

Jane couldn't understand that I was purposely trying to start unrest. She raised her voice in anger over what I was doing.

I accelerated the response. I informed her that in the future, if her session falls on my birthday, she would have to pay double my fee.

The venom poured out of her for about the next five minutes. When she was finished expressing all her emotions, she was gasping for air.

For the next few months, Jane wouldn't let go of what I had said about the new fee system. The miraculous aspect of this situation was that she realized she could verbalize these emotions, and I would not abandon her. As she felt more comfortable with this concept, she attacked herself less and attacked me more and more.

Months later, the eating disorder dissipated. It gradually decreased and stopped without any reoccurrence.

Before this intervention, Jane bottled up her hostility and avoided conflict. Battling with me, a person who she felt close to, helped her realize that strong emotions, when expressed properly, aren't bad and a good relationship can withstand conflict.

Words are only words; the importance is how one expresses them and how another person reacts to those words.

I wouldn't expect everyone to operate with this complexity, but I feel it would be great to have more people accept the verbalization of negative feelings without an automatic reaction of throwing negative emotions back.

> The ability to listen without reacting is an art.

Emotional Education helps people understand that verbalized critical emotions are misdirected energy and the listener should not take them to heart. Unfortunately when these feelings are redirected inside the individual, the emotions can cause serious health-related problems for the sufferer.

Often during sessions, Jane asked if I was disappointed with her for the way she spoke up to me.

I asked, "Are you saying that you were just annoyed or were you truly feeling that way?"

She responded that she was able to verbalize anger for the first time. This was a more progressive state than she had previously experienced.

During the time of her father's death, Jane stated only that she was disturbed with me but did not feel it. Now she was able to state it and feel it. She was coming in contact with not only the type of "poison" she swallowed as a child, but how it tasted.

I further explored how it would help her to know if I was vexed with her. She responded by stating "If I talked back to my parents the way I am talking to you, they would have been infuriated with me."

I then answered her question, "It's about time you talked back to me that way." This prompted her to tell me, "I understand now that you do care about me, and I feel it."

135

She continued to discuss if she was financially responsible for her birthday session. Now, I felt it was fine for her to feel valued. I stated that she did such a good job verbalizing her negative feelings towards me that she should be rewarded and she would not have to pay for that session.

She felt esteem, and was shocked that I was understanding and not punitive. I was able to reconcile Jane's past experiences and her present so she was able to move on and enjoy life.

Over the next few months, there was a marked improvement in Jane's behavior outside therapy. She no longer allowed her mother to contradict her or put a damper on her emotions. She found a boyfriend and created a more positive environment with her friends and colleagues at work.

The treatment had apparently taken her through a transition from a non-feeling to a feeling state, and to a positive environment which she could reproduce.

Treatment released the venom and personality change occurred. Jane became successful in life. She is able to express negative feelings towards others and is not afraid of others disapproving her emotions.

I've observed that many families have something in common when it comes to obsessive or addictive behavior.

The family is in denial and cannot face the real problem. The family sometimes resists seeing the person as who s/he is, and they pay attention to the behavior. Many times they talk only about the behavior as if the behavior has all the power—not the individual.

The family members only perceive how the behavior looks to others; thus, the addictive or obsessive individual doesn't feel cared for or understood. Therefore, the individual's hurt emotions

136

never heal.   He continues with his poor behavior pattern of addiction unless someone takes an interest in the person...and not the symptoms.

The addicted person needs to talk and the therapist or an interested party should just listen and not place his attitudes upon the addictive personality. It is a long process, but it a can eliminate the destructive behavior.

Favoritism

Successful communication is important in every aspect of life. The feeling of security in life can be instilled by just listening, discussing, observing body language and actions of others. Without it, people can become perplexed in their thoughts and actions and relationships can deteriorate.

Negative feelings are just as important as positive ones. Parents often silence negative feelings expressed by their children. This causes problems within the family structure. For most families, understanding and accepting a child for negative comments is a bizarre concept.

When siblings have difficulty understanding a parent's misdirected emotion towards them, it causes trouble for everyone. It is similar to a story of Cain and Able in the *Old Testament of The Bible*. Able was the father's favorite son.

Apparently Cain couldn't verbalize his jealous feelings, and he killed his brother by hitting him on the head with a stone. Perhaps, if Cain had been permitted to express his emotions about the favoring, he might have gotten his father's acceptance, and the murder might have been avoided!

I believe the energy an individual generates may eventually return to that person the same way as in the old expression, *What goes around comes around.* Cain became a builder of cities and died in a room he built when the stones caved in on him. It depicted the same way he murdered his brother—a blow on the head.

Favoring one child over another is quite common and sometimes hard to avoid in families. The scars and pain of non-favoring are carried with an individual throughout his life.

I have had families of siblings who were in pain from scarring memories of their childhood because these individuals were not the favored children. As a result, they felt resentment towards their favored sibling, and they felt anger towards their parents' actions and motives.

Typically, as children, they were not permitted to communicate their sad or angry emotions.

As adults with animosity over this situation, they usually ask, "Why would parents love one child more than the others?" They also wonder why parents deny that the favoring process occurred.

This unfair caring can lead to all kinds of emotional turmoil for the siblings in their adult lives.

My response is, "It has nothing to do with you personally. It usually has to do with the Story of your parents' Lives. Many parents are not aware they are behaving this way."

Parents often project an unfair relationship between their children because it is based on their own emotional attitudes left over from their childhood.

In the following case, parents dealt with the favored child the way they wished they had been treated by their own parents. Brenda, who was the non-favored child, experienced how the parents felt growing up.

Of course, the child doesn't understand this dynamic and is confused by their parents' motivation and behavior.

In addition, there is irony to this whole matter. All of my clients who sought therapy for this problem agreed with my theory and felt better after I brought the following observation to their attention. They realized that they were not the problem.

The favored child often doesn't turn out to have a better adult life or grow into an emotionally-responsible adult. If parents do so much for a child, he doesn't learn how to make his own decisions and take responsibility without his parents' advice.

My clients learned to handle responsibility because there wasn't anybody to stand by giving them advice. In the long run, the non-favored siblings were better off emotionally because they were trained by their parents to be independent people.

Still, the non-favored siblings must emerge from their childhood bitterness.

I tell my clients, "If you allow the anger to build up, it can lead to trouble. You should feel the displeasure, understand it, and move from it. You need to do what makes sense, and not act on how you feel—you cannot control how you feel just how you act.

Distract yourself; don't let your mind be pulled into the past. Spend time each day doing something that makes you feel good and keeps you in the present, whether it is reading, watching television, or exercising. Practice this concept for your lifetime; it takes patience to master."

BRENDA'S LIFE STORY OF FAVORITISM IN THE FAMILY

One of my clients had a serious case of favoritism in her family. Brenda's husband died when she was in her thirties. She was left with three young children to rear by herself. She is a tall, beautiful lady with dark brown hair and a lovely figure. She came into therapy because she was conflicted with a childhood history that dealt with favoritism.

At the time, Brenda was renting an apartment from her sister, Mildred, who was the *favored one* in the family.

Her family thought that Brenda came into money as a result of a life insurance policy on her husband. Mildred increased the rent on her apartment,

140

which my client couldn't afford. She told this fact to Mildred, who did not believe her.

The non-payment of the additional rent led her sister to take Brenda to court with the parents acting on behalf of the favored sister to collect the rent. This led to the eviction of my client with her young children. Brenda felt deep resentment towards her family.

I taught, through Emotional Education, that these feelings were unproductive and getting her nowhere. She moved on with her life instead of passing judgment on her family.

Brenda took on the role of trying to make her own life better instead of feeling sorry for herself. She found a new apartment and obtained employment.

Brenda leaned towards a positive environment, and didn't get pulled into the negative side of this terrible situation.

In spite of this turmoil, my client still wanted a relationship with her parents and sister.

I advised, "Don't talk about what happened after the death of your husband, even if your family wants to discuss it. Stay away from the negativity your family is radiating."

Brenda managed to establish a cordial relationship. She recognized that her sister did not have a better life because she was favored. "I have the power to support myself and my family without anyone's help."

This sense of empowerment gave Brenda a feeling of satisfaction in being an independent woman.

She is now working on the second phase of her Life Story. She is learning to be more relaxed when she sees or hears how other people are favored unfairly. She is realizing that it is a common occurrence.

It does not pay for her to become bothered when an unfair practice happens. Brenda is emerging from her childhood negativity.

She acknowledges that life is filled with problems, but she knows that she has the ability to change her outlook for the better. "I have to keep situations in perspective as to what is really important or what my real goal should be."

> *Positive emotions may have the tendency*
> *to be side-tracked if the person goes by his*
> *negative or hurt feelings rather than*
> *on an intelligent goal*
> *of what makes logical sense.*

Preferential treatment with special privileges goes on throughout life. Another example of favoritism has to do with a male client who has two older siblings.

KEVIN'S THEME OF "I'LL NEVER BE SUCCESSFUL"

Kevin is a good-looking man in his twenties with an athletic build. All through childhood his parents expressed a desire for his siblings to be successful.

However, my client's family gave him the impression that he couldn't become an accomplished individual. It instilled in Kevin a strong desire to triumph in everything he did. He wanted to prove to his parents that he should have been one of the favored children in the family.

142

When Kevin married, he had the love of a good woman and good fortune started to materialize when he felt truly cared for.

In therapy, I also generated this sentiment by listening to his endeavors and expressing words of approval.

Kevin became a successful coach, and determined to win a championship title for his school. He was still aiming at a childhood dream of being the favored child, but due to circumstances, he had to stop coaching for a while. He felt terrible and unfulfilled.

I reminded him that he was a rich man with a wonderful wife and beautiful children. I reminded him that many people can't claim this. Loving and caring people are what matters in life because money or awards do not make us rich. It is family and friends who make us wealthy.

Through some setbacks and trouble, he has learned his lesson about the true definition of success. Kevin's philosophy has changed since he has returned to coaching. Now he just wants to have fun with his team members. He has gained the understanding that accomplishments and happiness in life are not necessarily determined by the amount of wins and loses you have, but by the people who appreciate you.

Kevin, as compared to his siblings, was not supposed to be the successful one. He was an underachiever, acting foolish to gain attention. Now, not only do his parents have high admiration for Kevin, but he also has the respect of his entire family.

Favoritism doesn't exist only within a family environment. Favoritism exists everywhere—in the workplace, in your neighborhood, in community groups and every imaginable place you can think of.

143

People usually want to be the favored person in life because society believes this concept can help a person get ahead and do well in life. Being favored is a goal most want to attain. How can you go beyond this need?

It's okay, in my opinion, if you want to become more favored, as long as you use this position to be helpful to yourself and others. Should you use it for personal gain, it can result in downfall.

A THEME OF EMOTIONALLY FAVORING ANOTHER

I was working with a young married couple in their late twenties who wanted to buy a house from an elderly, widowed woman.

My clients reported that the elderly lady declined all the offers made on her home, and some of the offers were beyond her asking price. Listening to my clients' story, it appeared that this woman had difficulty separating from a house which had fond memories.

This couple really wanted the house but gave up because it became too expensive. The elderly woman was stuck in her past and I knew my clients could help her move on.

I asked, "Do you like this woman?"

They responded that they did.

I also asked, "Would you give this lady a standing invitation to come over to the house if she sold it to you with a price tag that you can afford?"

My clients responded in the affirmative, although they thought the idea was crazy. Why would the woman sell the house for a lower price?

I told them about the story of the boy in Harlem whose nose bled when he lost his gold cross. I explained, "Many actions an individual displays have an emotional component. Perhaps it doesn't make any intellectual sense to others, only to the person involved."

The young couple went along with my suggestion. They told the lady she would have an open invitation to visit whenever she wanted if she sold them her home for their affordable bid which was lower than the asking price.

It worked, and she sold them the house. The young couple became the favored people out of the population who wanted to buy her house.

The couple did not give her more money, but they gave the woman their compassion and understanding. The woman visited a few times and the family always welcomed her. The woman felt the young couple understood her dilemma of moving away from her home and memories. She felt cared for and understood by this couple.

It is not hard to become a favored person; you just must understand what the other individual needs emotionally. In the above case, the older woman wanted to sell the house but her inner being had an urge to stay with her memories.

The young couple relieved this woman of her tensions and state of imbalance. Thus, they received preferential treatment for their friendly, helpful consideration.

In the above situation, my clients did not make excuses for their trouble. You must look at a bad situation, analyze it, decide on your goals, and make your life better. You can learn from your hardships to achieve a successful outcome. The key is to recognize that you have strength and wisdom to bypass life's frustrations and fears.

145

> *The choices you make have the ability to define you.*

Don't dwell on self-pity; you have the ability to become a winner in life.

Some People Attract Trouble

Your negative mysteries cannot be kept inside your mind; they can fester and can poison your health and life. Some people try to use denial in order to change their reality. It doesn't work.

You must take on your problems to move on with your life. You might want a quick solution to a situation, but you cannot get a solution until you learn and accept the underlying cause.

> *If you really want to do something,*
> *you will find a way;*
> *if you don't, you will find an excuse.*

The story of Adam and Eve, from The Bible, can make you wonder if you are predisposed to or attracted to trouble, and this can be a hidden secret.

In the story, Adam and Eve had everything they wanted in the Garden of Eden, but they did not obey The Creator's rule to not eat the apple. They ate the forbidden fruit from the Tree of Knowledge and were expelled from the Garden.

In my experience, people generally know there is something not right about a circumstance yet they do it anyway. As human beings, do we attract trouble on an unconscious level?

While I was in Manhattan waiting for a subway train during rush hour, most people were looking down the tracks to see if the train was approaching. Some people hope that they have the ability to hurry life and perhaps they hope that they even have the ability to stop certain events.

I wondered, *Maybe these people think if they look at the tracks, they can make the train come into the station and get home faster.*

The train finally approached and at the same moment four policemen came down the stairs onto the train platform. They pulled out firearms.

A normal reaction to this event is that people would be afraid…but they were not.

In fact, as the train was moving into the station, the crowd of people started moving to the area where there was police activity.

I, on the other hand, started walking away from the activity. Four policemen with guns drawn didn't need my help. If there was any gunfire, I didn't want to get hit by a stray bullet.

Many people are attracted to drama because there is a thrill in the danger—or perhaps they get some gratification from other people's misfortune. Whatever the reason behind their motivation, it seems that many people don't feel cared for in childhood and this may explain why so many are fascinated by dangerous situations.

> *Most people do not realize that their behavior*
> *is linked to their Life Story,*
> *and they blame the present conditions*
> *for their actions.*

Using excuses helps people deal with their current reality so they don't have to face the deeper issues inside.

Life is full of irritations, and it is not the events themselves which are important but the effects on the individual.

The same experience can happen to two people at the same time, and only one becomes troubled over the situation. The result is an emotion called anxiety. Anxiety is a feeling which arises when inner tension is triggered. That anxiety seeks a path to escape…resulting in one's reaction to the occurrence.

JERRY'S LIFE STORY OF BEING THE RESPONSIBLE ONE

Jerry, in his early forties of tall stature and golden brown hair, only sees what he wants to believe. He is working on changing this perception.

For example, Jerry was at work when he had an altercation with his supervisor over an assignment. The supervisor wanted Jerry to finish the work that another co-worker neglected and left unfinished.

Jerry didn't want to accept the assignment because this situation had previously occurred at work with the same worker.

The supervisor threatened my client with insubordination and intended to write him up.

Jerry considered reporting the supervisor for unfair practices but instead, he walked away. When he calmed down, he started making sense out of the situation rather responding by how he felt. Jerry asked himself, *What can this situation and these emotions have to do with my Life Story?*

Jerry thought to ask himself this question because he felt he was overreacting. He tried to remember if these emotions and/or situation ever happened to him before, and it reminded him of his father's behavior.

Jerry remembered becoming angry when his father confronted him about a mess which was made by his younger brother. His father expected Jerry to clean

149

it up even though the father knew it was the brother's doing. In a few minutes, he traced the origin of his true anger with his supervisor to the Story of his Life.

People repeat the familiar story of their life until they emotionally learn it, and then they are capable of changing it.

> *When you are not sure if a situation*
> *relates back to your past, it is a good idea*
> *to ask yourself the following question:*
> *"Is this a new emotion I am feeling or an old one?"*

My client understood this idea after thinking back to his childhood. He realized the anger he felt towards his supervisor was based on his previous experience as a child.

By asking yourself the above question, you can affect the Themes in your life. Although you cannot change the past, it is possible not to relive or re-create it in the present or future. It is possible to do Emotional Education on yourself.

In our session, Jerry stated that I would be proud of him for the above intervention and I was. He said, "Understanding the story of your life really works."

It is my idea that if we do a better job of comprehending our hidden emotions and practice Emotional Education, our past history won't have to repeat itself.

Jerry realized that elevating his voice to his supervisor would not accomplish any successful outcome. He knew he should talk to his supervisor but in a soft manner.

Jerry approached him and asked if it was a good time to talk. The supervisor replied that it was.

He calmly stated, "I would be glad to follow your instructions to fix the incomplete assignment for my colleague if you want me to do so."

Jerry added, "If I do the assignment, will it really solve the problem with this employee? Would it help this co-worker learn to take responsibility to do a good job if I pick up the slack by doing it for him?"

Jerry made sure he didn't bring up any negative parts of the previous conversation by restating it wasn't fair to him to do another's job. He focused his questions on the responsibility of his colleague's performance...not on his supervisor's decision.

He knew he was approaching it in a way so as not to evoke hostility towards himself. He was also trying to avoid re-creating his childhood environment with his father. Jerry was working to change his Life Story.

His supervisor responded, "You make a good point; I wasn't thinking about the other employee's responsibility for finishing the assignment. I won't ask you again to do this."

As a result, Jerry reported that his relationship with the supervisor had improved.

About a month later, two more opportunities for insight into the story of Jerry's life were presented. He realized he was spending time going around correcting injustices wherever he encountered them, and began to feel that he was a modern-day Don Quixote.

151

Injustices bothered him. For instance, once he saw a construction crew tying up traffic while working in the middle of a busy street.

He felt the workers could move their equipment to the side and still perform their job. Jerry looked for a police officer to correct the problem.

He was annoyed by the lack of consideration shown by the construction crew and he knew their behavior was unfair to others.

Still, Jerry realized it didn't make sense to continue with his behavior and his conduct could cause him trouble with others.

He realized that his behavior to clear up injustices presented him with many confrontations which caused him stress.

He thought about how these injustices might have something to do with not feeling affection as a youngster because this theme was confronting him on a regular basis.

He understood he was trying to correct the unfairness in his personal life from his past; however, he was doing it in the present.

Jerry determined that it was okay to leave his past pain in the past, but it was difficult. He is currently working on his behavior of trying to distract his feelings by trying to correct the injustices he sees around him. He is trying to act on what is logical and not how he feels.

> *The development of an individual*
> *depends upon his struggle to apply*
> *his unproductive energy*
> *towards the most productive means.*

Another opportunity for Jerry's growth had to do with the recent death of his family doctor—a twenty-year close relationship. His death hit him harder than Jerry expected.

JERRY'S THEME OF LACK OF LOVING ATTENTION

He questioned the impact and tried to figure out what it might have to do with his Life Story. He recognized that he felt his doctor was more of a father-figure to him than his own father.

This thinking helped him get into contact with old stored emotions. He felt the loss and questioned, "How can I leave the past in the past and work on the present?"

He worked on this issue by telling the story of the doctor's death and his feelings towards his absentee father. He didn't dwell on his father's lack of emotion towards him; he just expressed his sad thoughts on the doctor's death.

Sharing that story helped Jerry to realize that his father was too much in denial to improve his relationship with his son. For the father not to be in denial, he would have to face years of neglecting his son.

Since this discussion, the relationship between Jerry and his father has not improved on the father's side, yet greatly improved for Jerry's mental health.

The world is full of unexpected twists and turns, and you must know yourself, accept your limitations, and get on with your life.

Sometimes you may try to re-create the familiar as Joe does in the next story.

153

Joe was a man in his forties, successful and intelligent. As a child, he grew up being relatively poor.

He reported to me that his parents used envelopes with written categories on the front where his father's paycheck was distributed. One of the envelopes was for rent, one was for utilities, one was for food, and one was for clothing.

No one in his family bought anything on impulse; the money was carefully doled out into living expenses.

Today Joe intellectually understands that he is doing well financially. Yet, he is afraid he may be poor again; in fact, this is his fear. His thinking is not logical because he is financially stable but he has to be careful in his actions not to create the old familiar environment of his childhood.

He had a tendency to make his anxiety come true, and it was his signal to himself that he was not functioning properly.

I brought it to Joe's attention he was trying to relive his worry of being economically strapped.

He reported, "I get so overwhelmed when I have to pay monthly bills that I procrastinate and pay them late."

Even though he knew he had money in his checking account, he let his feelings dictate his actions. He was constantly late in his payments, and he was charged with late fees.

Joe was making his past misgivings come true because he didn't see the obvious…that he was reliving unresolved issues. Sometimes a person cannot see the obvious because he is too close to it.

154

In Joe's case, his childhood environment made him believe he might be comfortable living in poverty.

I conveyed this reality and it started to make sense to him. Now he is working on paying his bills on time.

> *We go through life without realizing*
> *how powerful our inner struggles are*
> *and how much they influence our behavior.*

You may fool yourself and others about your true state of being, but the trouble is still present. Outside forces, such as a financial recession, may enhance your anxiety. One has to be careful not to turn the outside trouble into inner turmoil.

I have observed that when people are anxious, there is a tendency to pick an argument with someone. Should they become successful, the anxiety turns to anger. It appears that anger is a more comfortable state than anxiety for many people.

You are the one who causes circumstances to occur. What you cause to happen, how, and when depends on a great deal upon your motivation. You can learn to solve the conflicts and anxieties between your past and your present by being aware of your Life Story.

Don't Blame Yourself

Thinking and understanding about the Story of Your Life is a process that helps you to become enlightened about your own Being.

We have the power to change our lives for the better. Some of us find it hard to break away from the pattern of behavior we were taught through our early environment and role models.

Many of us find it difficult to understand ourselves and accept our limitations.

> *The motivation and truth of our past and our present*
> *are hard to see when it is in front of us,*
> *especially since we repeat*
> *the Story of our Lives with others.*

Avoid viewing repetitive behavior as unproductive in your development. Sometimes re-enacting your life can actually be helpful as a learning experience to move your life forward.

Therefore,

- stop degrading yourself,
- stop feeling sorry for yourself, and
- don't blame yourself for making mistakes in life.

It's just a learning experience which can lead to a positive outcome of accepting who you are as a person.

I feel, the way to master a concept is to go through it again and again in another period of time until you can learn from it and emerge successfully.

156

We are attracted to certain situations or people in order for us to duplicate some aspect of the Story of our Life.

The formula for getting away from trouble is: Do not go by how you feel just do what makes sense.

JEFF'S LIFE STORY OF UNFAIRNESS AND THEME OF FEAR OF LETTING OTHERS DOWN

A male client came to me for therapy. He was about thirty years old and an industrious individual. He asked, "I am feeling under the weather. Should I call in sick to work tomorrow?"

Before I could answer, he went on, "I would feel too guilty if I didn't go into work, so I should probably go to work anyway."

I asked, "What do you feel guilty about?"

Jeff explained that the people in his office would be disappointed if he didn't come in because another person would have to take on more responsibility in his absence. "It is unfair."

He remembered all the disappointments he felt as a child growing up, and he didn't want to do that to someone else. The Story of his Life with the Theme of letting down others was interfering with what he knew he should do when he was sick.

Jeff's Life Story was difficult. He was an unplanned pregnancy and his mother relied heavily on the older siblings to take care of him.

His siblings made him believe he was a burden and they blamed him for their circumstances. This emotion of unfairness haunted him throughout his adulthood.

157

Many times a person will hang on to an old way of behaving because he believes the circumstances make it difficult for him to experiment with new methods which might be gratifying.

I asked, "What will happen if you feel guilty and stay home?"

He admitted, "I would feel so accountable that I would punish myself by overeating to numb the pain." He asked, "What can I do about my negative feelings?"

I questioned, "What makes sense to you?"

In thinking logically, he said, "I should call in sick, and not punish myself by overeating." Recognizing that using his logical mind wouldn't alleviate the emotional struggle, Jeff asked, "What should I do with the emotions and my desire to numb the pain by overeating?"

As with many of my clients, I stated, "You can't control how you feel...only the way you act. Distract yourself with something else until the painful feelings pass." Jeff said he would try.

I admitted, "I know this concept sounds easy, but it is hard to practice. Nevertheless, with time the idea will become easier and easier to apply."

A person needs to understand that he might be unaware he is repeating his Life Story. He should not blame himself if his life doesn't work out the way he dreamed it to be.

Step back and think about what is happening in your life. You create your own reality by the choices you make, and the choices you make are fueled with past thoughts and experiences. Repression keeps the person in a continual state of confusion by preventing him from becoming aware of his memories, yet what is forgotten still remains an active energy in his mind.

158

This energy must be released in positive channels such as verbalization.

WILLA'S LIFE STORY OF PUTTING ONE'S NEEDS ON HOLD TO CARE FOR OTHERS

A female client was faced with a similar dilemma in the workplace. She was the only girl in a family of brothers. Her mother had been ill for some time and Willa knew that her mother was going to die. The mother raised her daughter to be responsible for others. The mother expected her daughter to take care of her siblings and father after her death.

Willa was a respectful daughter and she did what her mother asked her to do. She took on the job of caring for her siblings, her father, and taking care of the household duties—a big chore for any child.

Today Willa is a supervisor in a large corporation where she is in charge of an entire department. She is protective of the people she supervises as well as superiors.

The harder she works, the more projects she gets to do. In fact, she reports that she is always the last person to leave the office.

Unfortunately, no one compliments Willa on her extra effort; her superiors just expect her to do the job. She suspected that this reaction is similar to her father and her brothers' lack of appreciation towards her devotion to the family. Therefore, Willa believes no one really appreciates her sincere effort, and she feels that her staff thinks she is foolish for working so hard.

Even in the workplace, Willa is following the promise she made to her mother on her deathbed, and she has put her life on hold.

159

Working so hard, she had little time for a social life; she never married and sometimes felt lonely.

Her mind became a file cabinet of unsatisfied childhood tensions. Yet this storage area is not dead; it is alive and active. This experience is unfinished business for her and will not vanish until it is totally verbalized, understood and accepted.

On her job, these thoughts continue in the form of disguised work-related substitutes.

Willa is learning not to blame herself. She also acknowledges that she can't blame others for this dilemma. More importantly, she realizes that she has the ability to change. This clear understanding has enabled Willa to predict the probable results to her various ways of behaving.

RICHARD'S LIFE STORY OF GOING OVERBOARD TO ACCOMMODATE OTHERS TO AVOID BLAME

Another client was repeating his Life Story through his chosen career and marriage. Richard is a successful professional with a young family.

He was the youngest child in his family of origin, sent to bed earlier than his siblings. The apartment was small, and his bedroom was right next to the living room where the family watched television. He described the loud sound traveling into his bedroom as if the TV set was in his room.

As a child, he explained to his parents that he couldn't sleep with the noise and asked if he could watch TV with the rest of the family.

They demanded that he get back into his room and go to sleep. Richard felt isolated from his family

160

and this emotion stayed with him throughout his adult life.

In addition, he was criticized and blamed for occurrences, which he had no responsibility for.

Richard related that when he was seven years old, he was playing in the living room while his mother was in the kitchen preparing a snack. She was an anxious woman, and when she dropped a plate on the floor, she yelled out to him, "It is your fault the plate broke because you were making noise."

As a result of these two Themes, he has had difficulty sensing another person's true motives. This is largely as a result of so many mixed messages from his mother.

Understanding the Themes in Richard's Life Story has helped him to (1) recognize when he is being falsely accused and (2) no longer go overboard in accommodating others to avoid blame.

Some years later, Richard married a woman who complimented the Story of his Life.

People marry, to a large degree, someone who reminds them of the familiar: a person who represents a parent or someone else from childhood. Sometimes a person is aware of this attraction before he gets married, but most marriages are made up of people who are unaware of how the Story of their Life arises in their marriage.

It seems that my client needed to marry someone who—no matter how hard he tried to please her—transmitted that his efforts weren't good enough... similar to the messages that his mother gave him.

Richard's occupational choice for a living placed him out of the home for long periods of time.

161

He runs his own business, works six days a week, and also in the evenings.

Richard unconsciously picked a profession, which isolates him from his family. This correlates to his upbringing in being separated from his family. He is doing what is familiar to him.

Due to his absence from the home, however, his wife feels not cared for, no matter how hard he tries to please her.

This might be similar to his wife's Story of her Life with a feeling of abandonment due to being left alone for long periods of time.

They both needed to understand how their behavior tied into the story of the other one's life, and how it transmitted itself in their marriage. In my opinion, they needed to not blame each other for the familiar paths they followed, and act in a goal-oriented way for the marriage to have success.

The success of a marriage or relationship depends, to a large degree, on two people helping each other. They both have the ability to change and make the marriage work. It is the couple's perceptions of marriage which determines their actions and emotions.

> *One of the most important aspects in life*
> *is to understand your reality*
> *and to keep changing your images*
> *to correspond to it.*

The giving and accepting of love is a continuous experience in living. Love, its perpetuation and renewal, should always be there.

In relationships, people are attracted to someone who will complement their Life Story and how they perceive themselves.

162

When you have a poor image of yourself, you may feel that you don't deserve to be in a nurturing situation and others pick up these unconscious feelings by your body language. You might attract someone who is not acting in your best interests.

When you act in a positive-deserving way, you will attract someone who will be helpful and loving to you. It is in matters of love that individuals show the quality of their mental images, and how they handle the problem of trying to make reality and images correspond. When reality and images correlate in your mind, success in life can be accomplished.

Decide what you want to accomplish and what your goals are. Visualize and built the images in your mind as to what they would look like when achieved. After the pictures are there, work out the realistic steps to make the scenes a reality. It is not enough to just send the pictures out into the world, you have to put a plan into effect. You have to work at it.

FRANK'S THEME OF "THERE IS NO ONE OUT THERE FOR ME"

I worked with a good-looking young male who was a college graduate. This client felt there was no one suitable for him, and he was handling this situation in a negative way.

Frank reported, "I hate the dating scene and there is absolutely no one compatible with me." He stated that he feels insecure going to single functions, and shies away from others at these gatherings.

As an only child, he felt he had to be perfect because he did not want to disappoint his parents. Living under this pressure, he felt inadequate and uncomfortable in any setting, especially in a social arena.

163

He felt something was missing in his personality. Frank stated, "I don't feel confident but I try to act self-assured. I'm meeting some nice women now."

I emphasized, "You don't always have to believe something to do it; if it helps, just do it."

When Frank is radiating positive energy, women pick up on it and it is easier for him to meet amiable individuals. This idea sounds easy but you must practice it to be successful because it takes time for this idea to work. You need patience.

I recommended that Frank not place himself in situations with people who do not bring out the best in him.

> *Avoid negative people; they have the ability*
> *to demonstrate only discouragement and despair.*
> *Remember the Law of Attraction:*
> *positive feelings attract positive emotions and*
> *negative attracts negative emotions.*

You might get discouraged and rejected in life by others; this happens to everyone. It is not how many times you get knocked down, it is how many times you get up that counts. If you emerge from it, you will be a stronger person emotionally.

The successful man or woman is the one whose images correspond most closely to the norms of society. If you have a good self-image, others will view your actions as successful, and seek out your friendship. You are the guardians of your own humanity.

Are There Emotional Components to Cancer?

You might think that my following thoughts sound unscientific; I would not blame you. Yet, it has been proven that there is a mind-body connection to some illness. It is unfortunate that most doctors aren't trained in this field. They have been trained in prescribing medication to aid people. Pharmaceutical research is important but so is one's outlook in life.

Eliminating stress and anger will not cure every disease, but it can trigger a host of biochemical changes in the body including a boost to the immune system. Cancer is a disease that has touched my family, my friends, and my clients.

Some of these individuals lived beyond the expected life span that their doctors quoted. In several cases, these individuals have and had the ability to picture the disease disappearing from their bodies.

Some also imagined and mentally focused on things that could make them happy. They did not give into feelings of hopelessness by withdrawing from life. They didn't stop living; they went forward and maintained a positive attitude. They were able to turn their time of illness into one of strength and growth. Their good outlook helped them live longer.

According to medical doctors, cancer is characterized by an unrestrained growth of cells. In most cases, these malignant cells build up into tumors that compress, invade, and destroy normal tissues and, if untreated, usually lead to death.

Physicians state the risk of developing cancer is related to many things such as who you are (e.g. family history and personality/nature), where you live (environment), and what you do for a living (day-to-day activity and lifestyle).

165

Beyond these concepts, I was interested in why some members of a family develop cancer and others do not. They usually all have similar genetic background, environment, and socioeconomic status. What makes one person become a cancer patient and the other one does not?

It is my belief that if you cannot feel and express anger or stress, these emotions become internalized and it can make you ill.

Our good and bad memories,
whether they are from the past or from the present,
are always with us.

Everyone deals with these memories in different ways. It seems that how one is able to hide repressed anger may contribute to the development of malignant cells.

When you can understand your feelings, you can better cope with them in an appropriate way. It can be helpful to look deeply into your life and see what experiences might be creating your sickness.

Sometimes when you are depressed or feeling hopeless, your immune system is weakened and it does not fight disease as well as it could. Focus on what is enjoyable. Emotional healing can impact illness.

Following are examples of people who avoided personal exploration and couldn't face their Life Stories. They could not look into the eye of their inner stressful memories and acknowledge them through a positive lens. The cancer continued to grow because of hidden, unresolved emotions.

166

Most therapists get clients through referrals. One of my clients referred his friend to me. The referral was a middle-aged man who had terminal cancer, and was given six months to live. The referring person felt I might be able to reverse his friend's cancer through therapy. I worked with the client who was a forty-year old male for six months until he passed away.

As Walt began to tell me about his life, I was particularly impressed with one memory which was quite significant.

As a teenager, he smoked cigarettes against his father's wishes. He related a story, which occurred on a Saturday, and according to Jewish law, a person is not permitted to smoke on the Sabbath. Walt had a cigarette on that day, and he saw his father walking across the street headed in his direction. He swallowed the lit cigarette so his father would not catch him breaking a religious rule.

I was amazed he did this because a lit cigarette must have been painful.

I asked, "Why didn't you throw the cigarette to the ground?"

Walt felt it might elicit his father's attention. He didn't hesitate to state that his father would have taken off his belt and beat him within an inch of his life for disobeying this rule.

I asked him to reconsider this response, suggesting, "Maybe your father would have lectured you on the religious violation rather than hit you."

He once again stated, "There is no doubt that I would have been be severely punished."

167

I asked him to explain how he might have *felt* emotionally if he had been beaten.

He answered by saying his father would have been correct to strike him. When I asked him how he *felt* about it again, he didn't understand what I meant.

I explained, "Would you have felt sad, upset, or even angry with your father for hitting you, even though you thought your father was correct in his behavior?"

Walt responded, "I would not have felt anything at all."

In other words, he wasn't aware or in touch with his inner being which was non-responsive to any sensory impression.

Being a victim of childhood abuse, I understood all of the turmoil. As I became an adult, I realized I had denied the emotions of my abuse just like my client was doing.

As I went through therapy myself, I was able to verbalize some of my angry childhood emotions. I hoped this client could do the same.

Unfortunately time was against him and his cancer won the battle. It appeared to me that my client did not have a warm relationship with his father because—without experiencing severe guilt—he couldn't tell his father how this situation really hurt him emotionally.

My client could not confess his true "sinfulness" about the situation to his father.

Walt could not completely accept his father's religious beliefs, yet he could not move on with his life. The client internalized his feelings of misbehavior and anger rather than externalizing them. Walt could not escape his true inner sensations.

168

In my personal observation, there are emotional components to cancer, which makes some people more predisposed to the disease.

JUDY'S LIFE STORY OF INABILITY TO FEEL EMOTIONS WITH A THEME OF PROTECTING THE MOTHER

I had a female client in her late thirties, married with children. Judy couldn't break her ties to the past.

The client came into therapy because she believed she couldn't make sensible decisions without her older brother's advice. Judy wanted to break this behavior pattern. After speaking to my client a few times, I invited her brother, Hank, into a session with us.

It became apparent that their mother was unable to take responsibility with the children so she permitted the older brother to make judgments for his sister.

When Judy asked her mother a question; she responded, "Ask your brother."

Hank made a game out of this situation and admitted, "I enjoyed putting my sister through various trials just for my amusement."

After hearing this confession, I asked Judy, "How do you *feel* about your brother's response?"

She defended Hank and insisted her brother was working in her best interest at all times.

I asked again stressing the word *feel* in the sentence. "How do you *feel* about your brother's behavior?" Judy looked at me as if she just didn't understand what I was asking.

The faculty by which Judy perceived her brother's inappropriate conduct was not functioning properly. Her image of her helpful brother did not

169

relate to the reality. Judy's childhood environment had the effect of making her feel incompetent to make decisions for herself.

During the joint session, another interesting point came out about their childhood. When they were both young children, their mother attached a fifty-foot rope to their waists. The other end of the rope was tied to a tree in the backyard of their home.

The mother did this to be able to clean the house and watch her television programs without interruption from the children.

I asked my client how she *felt* about being tied up to a tree for hours.

Judy answered the question by stating, "My mother had to do what she did because she needed to be by herself at different times." She made excuses for her mother's poor nurturing skills.

I understood my client's point of view because I made excuses for my parents' poor behavior towards me. It is hard for a child to comprehend that his mother never wanted him, and this sentiment can last for his entire life if he doesn't accept it and emerge from it.

In therapy, we continued working on the concept of gaining insight as to the reason behind why she could not make decisions on her own. For months we dealt with this issue.

I decided to go out on a limb about her brother's insensitive behavior. I invited Hank back into a session.

In front of both of them, I stated, "Hank was truly negative towards you and sometimes he was intentionally hurtful."

I asked the older brother to confirm this statement and he did. "Why do you persist with this behavior pattern?" I questioned.

Hank replied, "I knew what I was doing, and I found it interesting just to see how far I could go with this mean conduct."

After listening to this comment, Judy still insisted that Hank was working in her best interests. She denied the non-supportive behavior.

It became evident to me that the only way to help my client was having her brother work on behaving in a more helpful role.

I asked Hank for support during Judy's therapy. It was a difficult task for Hank to be a positive influence; he was not to make choices for his sister, but to try to encourage Judy to use her own judgment. In this way, Hank could help Judy to improve her self-image. In fact, the only person who could build up Judy's self-image was Hank by giving his approval over decisions, which my client made on her own.

After about a year, Judy was able to make her own decisions and her brother gave up his non-supportive behavior.

Their relationship reached the point where they were both beneficial to each other. At this point, Judy mentioned she achieved what she wanted in therapy by having a good relationship with her brother; she was able to make judgments on her own, and she believed her therapy was completed.

I agreed that Judy was able to make her own decisions, but I felt she would benefit more if she was able to experience all her thoughts, especially negative ones. Not only was Judy unable to express such

171

thoughts or emotions, she could not even feel any anger or resentment.

I told her a story about a previous client who developed cancer and functioned in a similar way as Judy in that she had denied her feelings. I mentioned I was particularly concerned with people who didn't feel parental affection.

Judy said, "You are probably right; I should continue with therapy, but if I develop cancer, it will be alright because I miss my mother so much I don't mind joining her in heaven."

About a year later, I received a phone call from a person who was a friend of the above client. The friend told me that Judy didn't seem to be feeling well. She asked me to call her up and invite her back into therapy.

I did, but Judy stated that although it was a good idea to return she just couldn't do it.

It seemed that her past was too difficult for her to emerge from. She had tied herself so tight emotionally that she didn't want to—and couldn't—move forward.

Her friend called me a year later to let me know Judy had returned to the care of her mother in heaven. The friend mentioned how much Judy had missed her mother and that she died from breast cancer.

I asked myself, *Could there be a relationship between the Story of a person's Life and the development of cancer?* I have observed, in a few situations where women who have been exposed to continuous and hurtful rejections (divorce, abandonment, etc.) are more susceptible to breast cancer. This propensity is increased especially if they are not able to feel and verbalize their angry feelings.

172

It appeared to me that she didn't have enough time with her mother as a child. She was unable to move on with her life because of the vacuum she created by not confronting her inner self.

It is certainly overwhelming when cancer hits a member of your family.

My mother-in-law, I'll call her Sylvia, verbalized to my wife the thought that she would never live past the age of sixty-five.

My wife asked. "Why do you feel that way?"

The reason behind her logic was the fact that her mother passed away at that age. Sylvia was a constant smoker, and she knew the risks involved in continuing the habit.

At the age of sixty-four, she developed a continuous cough. Her doctors told her it was just a bad cold.

I tried to refer her to a different doctor. She stated that two of her doctors looked at her chest x-rays and reported she had a severe hacking cough. They prescribed medicine which did not help.

When Sylvia reached the point when she could no longer tolerate the painful cough, she accepted my referral.

She took her X-rays to the new doctor who—just by looking at the X-rays—diagnosed an advanced case of lung cancer.

When a person is afraid of something which is not based on any rational or medical information, he can unintentionally create an environment for the fear

173

to come true. It is as if he always knew it was going to happen.

I believe my mother-in-law's fear of dying at age sixty-five was really unintentional. Still, she was able to find doctors who gave her a diagnosis of bad cold instead of treating the real disease.

She was in denial about how bad her situation was and went along with the wrong diagnosis to fulfill her prophecy of dying at sixty-five years of age. Sylvia's history shaped and guided her decisions on her medical choices.

She was haunted by her own mother's death and had to relive it again. This time Sylvia took on the role of the dying mother, and my wife's role was the grieving daughter.

After an excruciating bout with cancer and a tremendous ordeal for my wife and children, my mother-in-law died at the age of sixty-five.

I asked myself, *Is it possible one can believe something can happen, and have the power to open the door for it?*

My mother-in-law couldn't emotionally break away from her deceased mother, and she had to re-enact the Story of her Life with my wife.

My mother-in-law felt my wife didn't understand the loss she experienced when her mother died in the 1950's. When my wife's grandmother died, she was a young child who had little perception of what death meant to the ones left behind.

When my wife was a child, my mother-in-law couldn't confront her loss verbally so she un-intentionally re-enacted it with her own daughter, which demonstrated to my wife the emotions of losing a mother at a fairly young age.

I believe there is a natural tendency in everyone to repeat the familiar even though he or she is not aware of it. In another situation, my wife and I

174

experienced how the Story of a person's Life intertwined with one's present life.

RACHEL'S THEME OF BEING CAUGHT UP
IN ANOTHER'S LIFE STORY AND SUPPRESSING ANGER

Rachel was a close female friend of the family and exceptionally beautiful. She could have been a top model; she looked like a Gibson girl with a perfect profile.

Rachel was an only child who grew up in a family in which her parents adopted one other child. Before the adoption, this boy lived in Rachel's neighborhood and the families were close friends. His natural parents died in a car accident, leaving him alone with no qualified living relatives who were physically able to parent the child. Rachel's parents adopted him, yet the child suppressed his emotions and never verbalized his loss or his parents' sudden death.

In a house, down the street, the adopted boy lived with his elderly, disabled grandparents under the supervision of Rachel's mother. According to the law in that state in the 1960's, the grandparents were too old and too ill to adopt such a young child.

The adopted child constantly visited Rachel's house with one problem after another. He came and went all day and night. Rachel was in the same age bracket as this boy, and they attended the same school. The adopted child constantly made trouble in school and in the neighborhood as well. Rachel could not escape him or the trouble he made. Most of her life Rachel was in denial about how she felt about these peculiar circumstances.

Her mother was overly stressed with this task, and under constant pressure with everyone's demands.

Previous to the adoption, Rachel's mother had medical problems which were so severe that occasionally she had to be admitted into a hospital. As the only child, Rachel had many household chores.

Her father was a man whose occupation took him away on business trips. Rachel had a short childhood and grew up fast.

At twenty-one, she married after graduating from college. Her marriage was a similar environment to her childhood home.

Her childhood thoughts and feelings were subconsciously familiar and comfortable to her. Rachel was unaware that she was repeating that environment, and did not do it intentionally.

On some level she wanted to correct the negative environment in which she grew up and to show others, especially her mother, that it could be accomplished without getting ill. Rachel started a family and was a stay-at-home mother.

Her husband had a high-powered job which took him out of town for long periods of time. In addition, he treated his job as his prime importance over his family.

When Rachel and her husband went out on a Saturday night, his cell phone rang constantly. Many of these interruptions left Rachel by herself in the restaurant or at weddings or dinner parties because he had to go back to his computer to fix a business-related situation.

For Rachel, it was a situation similar to the adopted child appearing at her door, unannounced, at unwelcome times. Again, she felt unacknowledged and not of prime importance.

It is amazing to me how the story of Rachel's life was being re-enacted, how she was able to accomplish it in an unintentional way, and be involved with someone—in this case her husband—to help her do it.

Obviously this could not have been planned on a conscious level.

> *The unconscious is so powerful that it can sense and attract the familiar.*

After a period of time, Rachel threatened to file for divorce. I believe on some level she felt that, because he loved her, the divorce proceeding would stop her husband from his negative behavior. It didn't.

The divorce was a stressful situation because her husband didn't want Rachel to get anything in the divorce. He wanted to call all of the shots; he wanted to be in charge of the situation.

During this period of time, he controlled the money. He was lax in court-ordered payments, and Rachel had to go back to work to support her son.

Her mother helped out by caring for her elementary-school age child. A few years later, her mother died and Rachel was left again.

Rachel's problems became overwhelming for her and on weekends when her child was with his father, she started to drink heavily. Rachel still could not feel or verbalize her hostility, and she hid her feelings behind a bottle.

She was invited to a house party of a friend and at this party Rachel met a gentleman. They dated and realized they had a similar problem with drinking.

They both joined Alcoholic Anonymous, and helped each other to recover.

Even at this time, Rachel blamed herself for the drinking problem; she never acknowledged any anger related to her childhood memories or her ex-husband.

Whenever she spoke of her past, it was with happy memories; she repressed her anger.

She continued dating Wilson. Unfortunately, she was diagnosed with breast cancer. She had a mastectomy and underwent chemo treatments. Wilson stood by her side and eventually they married with the loom of cancer over their heads. This man had true affection for her, and showed it. This was in contrast to her first husband who did love her, but didn't consistently act in a loving manner.

This loving care helped Rachel live beyond the years that her doctor quoted.

During her second marriage, Rachael viewed her cancer as a spiritually-transforming experience. She became religious and realized that all of life is impermanent. Through this process, she accepted her illness and talked about it freely, sometimes in a joking manner.

She used all her energy in being happy and looked forward to each day as a blessing.

During that time period, Rachael's father married another woman who appeared to only want his money. This woman bought new cars, a new home, jewelry, and designer clothes.

Rachel could not voice her annoyance with her stepmother's inappropriate conduct without causing major problems for her father. It appeared that history, once again, was repeating itself.

While the cancer steadily progressed, it took her years to *feel* any kind of disapproval towards her stepmother.

The anger was finally *felt* and verbalized at a dinner with my wife, her second husband, and me.

Rachel spoke angrily about her stepmother's wild spending sprees and that she did not take care of her ill father. She related a situation when her father was in the hospital, and the stepmother went out of state to visit her children.

Rachel felt helpless in the situation because she was undergoing chemo treatments. I believe this helpless emotion could be similar to the emotion she felt when the adopted child invaded her space.

It appears that Rachel's dilemma was her inability to realize her childhood memories had followed her into adult life. This pattern of behavior is hard to break.

Rachel's father died and she felt remorse and sadness. She had to accept it, and she had to accept how her stepmother treated her father.

In my opinion, she started to express this anger, but it came too late. She died from cancer two years after the death of her father. I heard after Rachel's death that her first husband told their children he felt remorse, and he was sorry for all the stress he placed upon their mother. He asked for their forgiveness.

Her second husband, Wilson, with his loving ways, kept Rachel alive for seven years while cancer spread throughout her body.

At the funeral home, some of the hospital staff came to the wake because they were amazed by her positive outlook on life. They felt her courage was an inspiration to all cancer patients, and they mentioned that she was always in good spirits no matter how much pain she was in. According to them, she was a pleasure to work with.

Your past environment contributes to what your present and future life can be like. You cannot choose your parents, but you can chose how you live. Remember the concept: *Your past is linked to your future.*

Question yourself on the theory: "Is it possible one's Life Story of not feeling cared for, feelings of abandonment, not feeling favored and denying that it happened could contribute to the onset of a terminal illness?"

> *Unless you can re-direct these emotions by feeling them, verbalizing and moving on, you cannot emerge from the negative part of your Life Story.*

Unless they are dealt with in a positive manner, a person usually has a tendency to repeat angry, negative emotions. It is important to have positive connections with others and strong emotional feelings that extend your life.

Discovering Your Life Story

Some people are attracted to unrest because of their Life Story. The truth about your life is facing you but sometimes you cannot see it. Your Life Story tells you where you have been and what you need to avoid and overcome in the future.

It's actually possible for a person to live in the shadow of an idea without fully grasping it. Sometimes you might have to learn a lesson over and over again until you avoid previously-learned negative behavior.

Many people get into difficult situations or relationships. They might be aware of it, on some level, but do it anyway.

Usually there is a split-second of doubt when something inside them says it is not a good idea. They ignore this inner message and move forward into trouble.

> *Don't blame yourself for that one minute of poor decision; learn from it.*

It might take a while to get out of a predicament or to get away from a person who causes you trouble. Patience and working with positive action can help.

Sometimes you realize how crazy a circumstance really was. You can see it clearly after you remove yourself from it. Most people cannot perceive a situation clearly while they are involved in it. It can be a very powerful experience, especially if it is a replica of a part of your Life Story.

Handling difficulty takes time to resolve. For some reason, I have seen that misfortune may take seven to fourteen years to come full circle and get resolved. It is similar to the story of Joseph in the *Old Testament*. Joseph had the ability to interpret the Pharaoh's dreams. One of his interpretations was that the crops in Egypt would have seven good years followed by seven years of famine.

The Pharaoh followed Joseph's suggestion of storing grain in the good years. When the famine came, there was food. I have observed the number seven and the number fourteen are significant to many people who are facing a severe dilemma.

Most people want an instant fix for their problems. People have a hard time realizing that no one has complete rule over their environment. This desire for control can cause more trouble.

True "control" is being comfortable when you realize you cannot completely dominate outside circumstances. You have choices and your destiny is not written in stone. It is important to believe in yourself and with patience you can eventually work towards a desired goal. Do this even if you don't believe in yourself.

Everyone has some sort of trouble in life, and your past is never truly behind you. These memories drift back into your life—especially the bottled-up anger from your past and the inability to confront the conflict.

> *It isn't the emotions themselves*
> *that create problems for you,*
> *but your inability to connect with them and*
> *eventually let them go.*

Before trouble occurs, you are in a state of repression involving a loss of memory for certain incidents, especially traumatic, painful ones.

Mr. D was a client who came into therapy because of a devastating financial situation where he invested in a business with someone who he thought really cared about him. He was a young father with two children under the age of ten and almost had to declare bankruptcy in the 1980's.

He kept questioning how he arrived in this situation. He knew he was fooled by another but couldn't understand why it happened.

I immediately thought the dilemma was associated to his Life Story, which was deeply imbedded inside his memory.

His bottled-up anger from the past and his inability to confront his conflict drove him into a circumstance of great emotional turmoil. The turmoil had to be acted out in his present life to release the pent-up energies.

His suppressed feelings were hidden from him and over the years they became clouded and distorted. These distortions influenced his behavior to get involved with someone who was not reputable.

As an adult, Mr. D did not want others to be in control of his destiny but he was in a situation where he had to rely on others for his well-being...just as he did as a child. He felt scared at this entrapment because it was similar to his childhood with his mother.

Whatever has gone wrong in our lives, whatever misconceptions or mistakes we have made, it is possible to move ahead, find satisfaction and comfort in our lives.

Through therapy, Mr. D knew he survived a terrible childhood with an abusive mother. The sense of helplessness did creep into his mind, but the feeling that he was a strong individual who survived past trouble was his source of hope.

It took Mr. D fifteen years to resolve his financial worries. While he was living through this nightmare, he didn't know it but it helped him to duplicate an important part of his Life Story which he hadn't been able to face.

He kept his childhood narrative secret in his unconscious; it was his hidden mystery. This situation assisted him to get the next level of development and move forward.

Mr. D's account can help people see for themselves that trouble is available to everyone even though we unintentionally recruit it. His plight placed him on the right track for the development of his life and soul.

Mr. D realized that he would have to deal with the past in order to move forward. No one can go back to his past to reverse what has happened. Looking back may not seem as if you are getting ahead, but these small regressed steps take you in the right direction.

Don't ignore the misfortune in your life because you can gain great wisdom from the experiences. Everyone experiences adversity but how you respond to your grief truly defines you.

Personal trouble should never define you as a failure in life because misfortune is a part of living. Sometimes it is hard to perceive that out of bad times there can be good outcomes. It is a life lesson.

What is painful to one generation is insight for the next.

Mr. D's inability to see his true childhood with honesty and inaccurately believing that his parents were loving and caring to him caused hardships throughout his life. Before therapy, Mr. D did not realize that he was harboring hostile emotions, and this denial hampered his well-being.

Mr. D related a memory from his childhood. Being the youngest and the weakest one in the family, his mother took her misery out on him. His early life was filled with stressful situations; he had to learn quickly to accept his mother's fury and adjust to it.

On one occasion, when he was nine-years old, his mother was in an extremely bad mood. She complained, "All I do is work, shop, cook and clean."

Her ability to shift her inner conflicts from a situation to a person was her way to deal with displeasure. This action permitted her to redirect her emotion into impulses. She reached the point of exasperation which turned into rage.

She took the lamp off the round wooden table. She turned the table upside down.

Before the child realized what she was doing, she forced him to the floor and started pounding the table into his chest. He tried to grab the legs of the table to pull it out of her hands. She was so strong the only thing it accomplished was that she lifted him up with the table and pounded him even harder.

He let go of the table feeling helpless, defeated and his whole body ached. She continued pounding on his chest until she was exhausted. His father and sister were standing, watching, during the entire incident.

His father said, "You could have killed him." Everybody walked away to their corners in the apartment and left him on the floor sobbing.

185

He stayed on the floor unable to move and hardly able to breath for about a half an hour. The pain in his chest was excruciating, and he felt close to death.

Mr. D repressed his childhood feeling that no one would protect him.

Remembering negative experiences isn't an easy task. In order for Mr. D to get healthier, he had to take this unpleasant journey. So many memories flowed through his mind, it became hard to process all of them.

He realized that he re-enacted his childhood of being cornered and made miserable by another. His business advisor was similar to his lying, manipulative mother who constantly said that she loved him.

Mr. D had to relive his past memories because he didn't acknowledge his parents' true uncaring attitude towards him.

Mr. D's habit was his inability to accept his past, yet he was *not made of Teflon* and these hidden, angry memories did stick to him. His hidden childhood despair caused Mr. D to attract similar situations in his adult life.

The type of trouble Mr. D found himself in was a business transaction that went terribly wrong. The particulars of this transaction are interesting.

At that time, for some unknown reason, Mr. D encountered an emotional connection with his business partner.

The partner told Mr. D many times that he was like a brother to him. His business partner wanted him to be successful in life; therefore, Mr. D felt cared for.

186

Mr. D also felt his parents looked out for him and loved him, but the truth was his hidden enigma in his subconscious.

Mr. D was being manipulated and deceived again. During this time period obstacles from his past were clouding my client's ability to see the true intentions of this so-called investment.

The project was initiated and a loan was obtained from a local bank. When Mr. D and his wife were sitting down to sign for the loan at the bank, his wife asked their attorney if they should have a business contract with their partner.

The lawyer stated that it wasn't necessary because the bank would watch for the loan as the project developed. He said that the bank would protect its own interests and at the same time, the bank would be watching for their best interests.

The lawyer Mr. D used for the loan misled him in a similar fashion as his mother did because the lawyer did not insist that the young couple should have a written contract.

The amount of difficulty someone may encounter is related to the themes from the Story of his Life. One's past enables the individual to be attracted to the familiar even if the familiar has negative impulses.

My client was a latchkey child long before the term was being used on a regular basis because he was left on his own for long periods of time. He was basically a child who no one cared for.

Mr. D had the potential to get into difficulty if he didn't watch out for himself.

The business situation had nothing to do with his intelligence. He was operating on his emotions, not what made sense. As a child, he grew up with an attraction for distress; it felt familiar.

The straw that broke the camel's back occurred during Christmas week when Mr. D received a lien by certified mail. At that time, he didn't know it but a lien can be put on a person's property for any type of defaulted loan.

He questioned himself, *Where is my money? I paid my bills that I was aware of, so what happened? How did I become responsible for all of the bills?*

After the lien was served, the bank that held his loan became defunct.

According to the local newspaper, this bank made loans that were not totally secured by collateral and another bank took over the problems.

The bank which was supposed to watch over his project left my client by himself in terrible circumstances.

The bank was acting like his father during his mother's beatings…just standing by and not reacting.

When Mr. D started to play the game of business, he was unaware of the rules and his lawyer never informed him of these dangers. The lien was for a large amount of money, which he didn't have.

He called his attorney to tell him what was happening, and the attorney seemed to be surprised.

Communication between the partner and Mr. D broke down, and my client's attorney said that he would handle it. He, too, couldn't resolve the issue. The business partner did not want to take any responsibility for the situation.

188

Mr. D had used his present home as collateral for the loan. He was in danger of losing his current home, or he might have to go into bankruptcy. He tried to talk to the new bank personnel to resolve this issue to no avail.

He had to pay off the debt by borrowing money from his in-laws to save his home. Now he had to repay two loans at the same time.

No one likes to lose power over any situation; we feel it is a sign of weakness and it makes us feel we are not qualified or experienced people.

There are times when circumstances take power over a situation, and it makes us feel scared and insecure.

The traumatic events drastically upset his wife and children with the possibility that everything could be lost.

As if this wasn't enough, he was pursued by even more anxiety. Over the next few years, his wife's health started to suffer. Many times his wife exclaimed, "I can't even look at the bills."

Her emotions were so powerful that she manifested more medical conditions. She experienced flashes of light followed by the sensation of a curtain across an eye. The feeling caused partial vision in her right eye. She became a victim of a detached retina of the eye, which if not surgically treated, causes blindness.

Shortly afterwards, she developed cataracts in both of her eyes. Cataracts are a growing opaqueness in the lens of the eye. The danger is the loss of vision until it is surgically removed and replaced with new

189

lenses. The stressful situation they were living under caused his wife to have a medical scare.

The pressure was building up in his life. Mr. D related that the situation involving their house caused his wife to verbalize angry feelings towards him for getting into this predicament.

Her reprimanding was hard for him to bear but it helped her release her inner hostile emotions. There were times Mr. D felt like leaving but he knew he didn't want to repeat the same situation he had with his father who left him crying on the living room floor after his mother's rage.

He followed my advice not to act on his feelings, just to feel them and understand the situation.

One day, Mr. D had to break into his mother's apartment because she hadn't answered her telephone for three days. She had fallen on the kitchen floor and was immobilized.

Before this incident, he had asked her many times if he could have a set of keys to the apartment. She didn't want to give him the keys because she entrusted the keys to her twenty-year-old granddaughter.

After his mother's fall, he learned that his niece had a tumultuous history. As a teenager, she was transferred to a special high school for children with conduct problems.

She was barred from her parents' co-op apartment, and started to live with his mother. In her twenties, she moved to her own apartment.

His mother said, "My granddaughter, Debbie, is very helpful because she calls me daily and comes over to my apartment every weekend to keep me company."

Thinking back to her comments he wondered, *Where was Debbie when she was lying on the kitchen floor for days?*

I explained to Mr. D that Debbie only cared for his mother when she could get something from her; it wasn't genuine.

His mother told him a story regarding his sister and brother-in-law. They fled New York City to an unknown location because they were afraid of their daughter's violent temper.

Looking back at some of these situations, he finally began to realize that he really did not come from a normal family. His mother had given the keys to her apartment to a person with a severe acting-out problem because she thought she would watch out for her.

His sister was running away from violent circumstances like his father did in my client's childhood. Mr. D recognized that he came from a family suffering from irrational thinking.

The pressure never let up. Shortly afterwards, his father-in-law became quite ill with congestive heart failure. The investment bills were still rising. His wife made plans for her elderly father but because of the financial circumstances she could not implement them. She felt guilty because she could not help him financially. Within a year, he died from pneumonia in a nursing home.

Mr. D's marriage and his life were strained to the hilt. He was paying off debts and working two jobs. Mr. D finally told his wife to stop yelling at him for something he couldn't see coming; otherwise, "I might get ill."

191

She couldn't stop focusing on all of the stress, and my client sensed even more pain was coming his way.

After a few more months of feeling unappreciated, one Saturday night he started to feel chest pains and pain going down his left arm.

His wife insisted he call his internist who told him to get to the emergency room right away. An angiogram was taken, and it was determined he had a ninety-percent blockage in his right coronary artery. He needed an angioplasty or his health could be in more trouble.

Six months prior, Mr. D's stress test determined he had no blockages. Mr. D asked the cardiac surgeon, "Can you determine how old the blockage was after you performed the surgery?"

It appeared that my client formed the blockage after the stress test, and it was around the same time he asked his wife to stop blaming him or he might get ill. After his surgery, she eased up on her hostile feelings.

Mr. D questioned, "Did I cause this terrible situation to occur?"

I explained that he didn't intentionally cause it, but that he needed to experience it emotionally.

He started to make connections. Looking back, the bank was only concerned with getting paid and not helping. "Did this have something to do with my Life Story?"

When he was a young boy, he had been abused many times by a cruel mother. Now he was feeling the same response he had as a child when his mother pounded the table on his chest; he felt he could die.

His father walked away and left him on his own. "Could I have unconsciously repeated my familiar Life Story? How could I have been unaware of it? How can an educated person recreate the obvious familiar situation?"

In his opinion, he did just that. The coincidences were too similar to think otherwise.

It was hard for him to believe he was able to block out the discomfort from his childhood. He intellectually understood his unhappy childhood but he didn't remember how it *felt*. He had to recreate it again.

His image of a tender, loving mother was a delusion in his mind—reality was showing him the truth. His mother fooled him for years because verbally she said she loved him. He needed to see the truth of her actions.

During the financial dilemma, Mr. D placed his mother in a lovely adult home. One day, his mother lost her balance and fell. According to her account of the situation, she was trying to go around a man who was struggling with his walker. She couldn't wait for him to walk through the doorway so she pushed ahead of him which resulted in her falling down. The fall resulted in no damage to her body.

Yet, she could not see the accident was caused by her own means. She stated, "I am waiting for an opportunity to trip this man so he can also fall." She had no sympathy towards others. Some older people mellow in life but his mother was incapable of it.

Mr. D told another story about his mother when she was in her eighties. He tried to talk to her about his childhood. He mentioned to her it was difficult for him to withstand her beatings. He told her that he managed to forgive her for her behavior.

She exclaimed, "None of those things ever happened; it must have been your imagination. I gave my life to you."

He wondered, *Was she capable of blocking out her relationship with me or did she feel she was a great mother?*

During his session he asked for my comments on the questions that had been going through his mind.

I mentioned that I thought she was aware of what she had done but she, once again, wanted to mislead him as to what really happened. She would benefit if he believed her. She did not want to hear him speak in a way that implied she was guilty of any wrong doing or abusive behavior.

In her nineties, her health rapidly declined and she ended up in the hospital. She complained that one of the air vents on the ceiling was blowing directly on her. Mr. D improvised with a piece of cardboard that deflected the air so she would be comfortable.

She thanked him and said, "You know I always liked you but I never loved you." Her statement surprised Mr. D because he imaged that she always loved him unconditionally."

His mother was transferred from the hospital to a nursing home. He still visited her and watched over her care. During one of his visits, an aid walked by and greeted her.

His mother asked Mr. D for some money. It confused him, "I don't understand your need for money."

She replied, "People won't do chores for me unless I give them money."

He asked if the other patients were tipping the help in the home. She said, "No, but I want the money just in case. When I look at people, I am always thinking what I can get out of them, and I know they are thinking the same way."

Her statement *hit him like a ton of bricks.* She was only concerned with what she could get from people or what they could do for her. This was the way she treated everyone and it didn't matter if it were her son or a stranger.

During this period of time, she knew about his dilemma with the investment project, and she never verbally expressed concern over the matter.

After these episodes, he finally understood that his mother was an extremely selfish and unloving person. It was difficult for Mr. D to accept that his made-up perception of his childhood was a lie.

Mr. D realized that his mother was a person incapable of any tender emotions. As an adult, he had to purge himself of this poison.

A family's role is to help its members, but he was raised in a house of strangers who were incapable of caring or helping each other.

The situation with the bank and his business partner forced him to learn, to accept, and to acknowledge the real pain of his unloving childhood family.

Before this experience, his wife told him that his mother wasn't capable of loving anyone. He could not understand emotionally what she was saying.

He had to relive and *feel* the truth. He realized the new traumatic experiences are painful but the old ones could never heal until he accepted and acknowledged them.

After many years, Mr. D was able to pay off the debts. His family travelled a long and difficult road to get out of pain. Through patience, they were able to emerge from the difficulty. The most meaningful lesson of this dilemma was the loss of money wasn't as important as losing his family.

Mr. D thinks of this nightmare as his personal awareness to the truth about his Life Story. He was able to find himself.

Before the loan situation, my client felt his life was on track. This period of time reenacted the trouble he faced growing up. The negative experiences were festering inside of him, and he needed to release its energy.

He could only lie to himself so long about his parents' behavior. His ability to deny what they were really like didn't change the truth about the nature of their unsympathetic behavior towards him. He was denying his childhood reality and denying it did not change the truth about it. Mr. D was a person who kept these memories in denial but was eventually able to purge himself of them and move forward with his life.

It is hard for a person to perceive the truth about a parent who only claims to love him. When one confronts the fact of this betrayal, it can be too painful to process.

In retrospect, Mr. D was looking for someone or something to take his mother's place as a caring individual. Unfortunately, or perhaps fortunately, he discovered someone and a situation similar to his childhood to reinforce the unloving and unsympathetic feelings he had as a child.

The realization was hard to accept but he finally admitted it. Betrayal comes to everyone and the path to recovery is less clear and defined. Some betrayals in life are so deeply rooted in your inner being, it takes time to repair them.

Remember the old adage, "Time heals all wounds." You must be patient. It appears you must muddle through it until you arrive at the end of the path to rebuild the lost trust.

Negative childhood memories make a deep impression in your subconscious. In some cases it has to be revisited in your adult life to move on. Sometimes a step backwards equals two giant steps forward in the comprehension of your Life Story so you can move forward in life.

Ending Thoughts

You shouldn't be afraid of the word trouble because in going through it you may find yourself. Trouble should be confronted so you can have new hope in life.

Aristotle stated that we are what we repeatedly do. Excellence, then, is not an act, but a habit.

In my observation, you may have good habits but the bad habits can keep you from achieving your goals. Bad habits can also place you in an unwanted pattern of behavior. You must work on building and creating a positive environment.

Live your life to the fullest even though you may enter into a negative period of time. Work on getting out of the negativity even though you might be afraid of it.

Emotions cannot control your life; remember, you have the power to overcome them. You must *feel* the anxiety but act on what makes sense and not on how you feel. Force yourself to be aware of what makes you afraid and try to avoid giving into the mishap.

Trouble has the power to infect your mind and make you sick if you let it take charge. You have the ability to confront the stress and comprehend its origin.

> *You can be your own superhero.*

Stop looking for people or using excuses to rescue you. You have the power to do it yourself.

Understanding the familiar Themes in your life is helpful. There are no easy solutions in conquering your fears and troubles. You may try to re-create a negative environment because (a) you have not fully recognized or accepted it and (b) it is a familiar pattern of behavior.

When you are reliving it, you might be unaware of the situation which you have created from your past. Your past is what shapes you and guides you throughout life. Your past resurfaces many times in a lifetime. Understand it, and you will not become a victim of self-pity for too long.

Anytime you have a fear of something, ask yourself, "Am I trying to re-create a familiar past experience? Is this new dilemma or an old one?"

Knowing these answers can help you understand where the origin of the turmoil is coming from. If you want to be a winner in life, you have to go back to the root of your issues.

When you repeat some of your old experiences, you can grow emotionally with what you learned from them. If you can understand what went wrong, you can avoid making the same mistake. You are not a failure if you don't give up trying to understand the source of the difficulty.

> *To understand the cause,*
> *you have to look backwards*
> *in order to move forward.*

You should not place yourself in a state of anesthesia. You might deny the negative parts of your Life Story, and usually when this occurs you cannot see the truth behind your actions. You might try to fool yourself, and stay in denial because the truth scares you.

It is not necessarily reliving memories that cure an individual. It is overcoming the resistance that helps a person move forward.

199

You might become involved in a terrible situation to emotionally learn a lesson. If you understand how and why you got into difficulty, it can enhance your inner being and life.

You might blame yourself about what could have been or what should have been. In fact, you can replay this tune over and over again in your mind.

Some of us believe we can hide the past from ourselves, and therefore, we attempt to change our Life Stories in our minds. Yet, we are only human and this ability is not within our dimension. Eventually the truth reappears.

Stop hurting yourself with the belief you might be a failure. Look forward to the future with bright thoughts of what you would like to accomplish.

Force yourself to emerge from negative outcomes by identifying the conduct you want to stop and ask this question, "Does this behavior benefit me?" Consider what else you can do which would help form positive ideas and goals. Decide which of these new ideas and goals you might be willing to try.

If the first one doesn't work, try something else. You always have choices. Repeat to yourself, "I can visualize a positive outcome in my mind, and I can work towards these ideas and goals until it is accomplished."

> *Your most important decisions today*
> *can become part of your past.*

So decide in which direction you would like to head—repeating negative experiences or making new positive experiences.

Perhaps one of the most interesting features of your Life Story is the degree in which you encounter

200

turmoil. Put aside the denial of hidden secrets; you must face the world. You can only lie to yourself so long before you realize you are not becoming a winner in the game of life, and you are not growing emotionally as a person.

Having regrets about yourself and your circumstances don't have any productive purpose in your development. Don't dwell on feeling remorseful and continue on your journey through life even though you can be faced with trouble at some point.

Life is not a spectator's game; it is an action game so you have to participate. Practice on what makes sense and not giving into how you feel. This simple concept can give you a richer life.

Only look back to your past to understand the topics in the Story of your Life; otherwise look towards the future for the positive aspects that are ahead of you.

You have the ability to choose the people you want to live with for the remainder of your life. You do not have to be associated with people who are toxic.

Don't let people or situations negate your success. Even though you have failing moments, you are not a failure as a person. Develop positive thoughts to replace negative ones. Repeat positive thoughts to yourself. When positive phrases are repeated, you are more likely to achieve your goals.

> *The positive words you say to yourself*
> *are essential*
> *to creating a successful mind frame.*

I helped my clients get rid of their inner negativity and poison that had been festering inside.

It is my hope that in this book I have assisted you in getting an idea of the sources of your trouble, how to handle and accept them.

There are various reasons why people have trouble in life. It might be helpful for you to realize that feeling memories, understanding them, and resolving them could help you to see how to take your negative experiences and turn them into positive ones.

The key to overcome getting caught in the past is to discover the Themes in the Story of your Life. The Gospel according to John says, "Ye shall know the truth and the truth shall set you free."

CPSIA information can be obtained at www.ICGtesting.com
Printed in the USA
BVOW06s1324010716

454261BV00013B/71/P